WOMEN WRITERS OF CHILDREN'S CLASSICS

Mary Sebag-Montefiore

© Copyright 2008 by Mary Sebag-Montefiore
First published in 2008 by Northcote House Publishers Ltd, Horndon, Tavistock,
Devon, PL19 9NQ, United Kingdom.
Tel: +44 (0) 1822 810066 Fax: +44 (0) 1822 810034.

British Library Cataloguing-in-Publication Data
A catalogue record for this book is available from the British Library

ISBN 978-0-7463-1152-3 hardcover
      978-0-7463-1157-8 paperback
Typeset by PDQ Typesetting, Newcastle-under-Lyme
Printed and bound in the United Kingdom

Contents

Biographical Outlines

JULIANA HORATIA EWING (1841–1885)

1841	3 August: born at the Vicarage, Ecclesfield, Cheshire, to the Rev. Alfred Gatty, Vicar of Ecclesfield, and Margaret Gatty (née Scott), second of ten children (two died in infancy).
1841–67	Educated at home, tells stories to siblings, works as hard as any curate in the parish.
1856–62	Edits family magazine: *Anon*, then *Le Caché*, finally *The Gunpowder Plot*.
1861	Contributes to Charlotte M. Yonge's *Monthly Packet* (published in book form with other stories in 1862 as *Melchior's Dream and Other Tales*). Spends earnings on taking two sisters to the seaside at Whitby for a month.
1865	Writes 'The Mystery of the Bloody Hand', published in the *London Society* magazine, an uncharacteristically gothic short story, never repeated; and *The Brownies*. Spends earnings on taking eldest brother on holiday to Holland and Belgium. First mention of Alexander (Rex) Ewing – in Mrs Gatty's diary.
1866	At the suggestion of Bell, her publisher, Mrs Gatty becomes editor of *Aunt Judy's Magazine*. Beginning of Juliana's regular contributions. Engagement announced to Rex Ewing, to her parents' consternation.

1867	1 June: marries Rex Ewing at Ecclesfield Church; 8 June: sets sail with her husband to Frederickton, New Brunswick, Canada.
1869–77	Return from Canada to settle at the army barracks at Aldershot; Ewing's most prolific period of literary output.
1873	Death of Mrs Gatty.
1877–9	The Ewings leave Aldershot for short-lived army postings around England.
1879	Rex sent to Malta. Ewing attempts to join him; gets as far as France, when ill-health drives her back. She has no settled home, but changes lodgings frequently.
1881	Rex is posted to Ceylon.
1883	Rex returns. They settle in Taunton at the Villa Ponente.
1884	The Rev. Alfred Gatty, aged 71, marries Mary Helen Newman, aged 47.
1885	13 May: death of Ewing at Trull, near Bath, aged 44.

MARY LOUISA MOLESWORTH (1839–1921)

1839	29 May: born in Rotterdam, the third of seven children, to Charles Stewart and Agnes (née Wilson).
1840 or 1841	The Stewart family return to England, to a small urban house in Manchester.
1840s	Visits to relations in Scotland, including her mother's mother, Nancy Wilson, a skilful story-teller. Educated at home.
c.1854	Taught by the Rev. William Gaskell. The Gaskells were neighbours in Manchester and apparently Mrs Gaskell encouraged her to write.
1855	The Stewarts move to a larger house, further away from Manchester's centre.
1856	First published work, the translation of a short story, 'The Bird-mother', in a magazine.

Late 1850s	Educated in France and Switzerland for two years.
c.1858	Charles Stewart, steadily growing richer, moves further out of Manchester, to Whalley Range.
Probably 1859	On a visit to Scotland, meets Richard Molesworth, a soldier, son of Capt. the Hon. Anthony Molesworth, and nephew of the 7th Viscount Molesworth.
1861	24 July: marries Richard at Grosvenor Square Church, Manchester. Follows Richard to army postings.
1862	Birth of Violet at Whalley Range.
1863	Stationed at Aldershot. Birth of Cicely, at Whalley Range.
1864	The Molesworths rent Tabley Grange, a large house, from Baron de Tabley, whose son, a poet, John Warren (1835–95), becomes Molesworth's secret, close friend from 1868 to 1871.
1865	Birth of Juliet at Tabley Grange.
1867	Birth of Olive at Whalley Range.
1868	Begins a novel; burns the first part three times. Charles Stewart moves to his grandest house, West Hall, very near Tabley Grange.
1869	4 April: death of Violet, aged 7, of scarlet fever; 7 May: Molesworth, in great grief, lets her house; 13 August: birth of son, Richard, at West Hall. Autumn: publication of novel, *Lover and Husband*; 20 November: death of baby son.
1870	Begins building new house, Westfield, near her parents.
1871	Birth of Bevil.
1872–4	Publishes three more three-volume, adult, novels. All sink more or less without trace.
1873	Birth of Lionel. Death of father, Charles Stewart.
1874	Westfield sold. Richard retires from army. Move to Wales.
1875–1911	Molesworth pours out over 100 books. Her first children's book, *Tell Me a Story* (1875), short stories which include an account of Violet's death, is well received; her second, *Carrots* (1876), and third, *The*

	Cuckoo Clock (1877) are runaway successes, establishing her as a leading children's writer.
1878	Moves to Pau, France; then to Caen.
1880	Separation from Richard. Molesworth, her children and her mother move to Paris.
1883	Molesworth's mother dies.
1884	Moves to 85 Lexham Gardens, London, with mixed feelings – it is too far out for friends to visit.
1890	Moves to Sumner Place, off Onslow Square.
1898	13 March; death of Bevil.
1899	Her final move to a flat in Sloane Street, with youngest daughter; all the other children now married.
1900	Death of Richard Molesworth.
1916	Death of Lionel.
1921	20 July: death of Molesworth, aged 82.

FRANCES HODGSON BURNETT (1849–1924)

1849	24 November: born at 141 York Street, Cheetham Hill, Manchester, third of five children of Edwin Hodgson, a general furnishing ironmonger and silversmith, and Eliza (née Boond).
1852	Family move to a bigger house.
1853	Death of Edwin Hodgson. Eliza runs the firm herself.
1855–64	Eliza, short of money, moves her family to Islington Square, Manchester, a just-genteel area, bordering poor backstreets.
*c.*1855–*c.*1863	Frances educated with her younger sisters, Edith and Edwina, at the Select Seminary for Young Ladies and Gentlemen, run by the Misses Hadfield.
1865	Eliza sells her husband's firm, unable to make it pay, and moves her family to Tennessee, America, to join her émigré brother. The Hodgsons are extremely poor. They make friends with the local doctor's family, the Burnetts. The doctor's son, Swan, falls in love with Frances.

1868	Beginning of her career: publication of romantic story, 'Hearts and Diamonds,' in *Godey's Magazine*.
1869	Family move to Knoxville. Frances publishes stories in increasingly prestigious magazines.
1870	Death of Eliza. Swan wants to marry the reluctant Frances.
1872	She travels to England; agrees to marry Swan on return.
1873	Marriage.
1874	20 September: birth of Lionel.
1875	Move to Paris where Swan continues his medical training.
1876	5 April: birth of Vivian. Burnett begins serial published in *Scribner's Magazine*, *That Lass o'Lowrie's*, the book that brought her fame. Autumn 1876: return to America; move to Washington, where Swan sets up as an eye and ear doctor.
1877–85	Grows famous, producing well-reviewed adult novels; frequently ill with strain, and frequently stays away from home.
1885	Vivian inspires Burnett to write *Little Lord Fauntleroy*, published in 1886, her first children's book, setting her on the path to huge acclaim and fortune.
1887	Burnett takes boys away from Swan to London, Paris and Italy.
1889	Boys return to father in Washington. Burnett takes house in Lexham Gardens, London (same street as Molesworth), busy with play versions of her books. She meets Stephen Townsend, aged 29, a doctor and would-be actor.
1890	Fetches Lionel, ill with tuberculosis, and searches, with Stephen, for cure in Europe. Lionel dies in Paris in December.
1893	To England again.
1893–1923	Crosses Atlantic twenty times.
1898	Divorces Swan.
1898–1908	Rents Maytham Hall, Kent; its walled rose garden inspires *The Secret Garden*.
1900	Marriage to Stephen Townsend.

1902	Leaves Stephen Townsend.
1905	Becomes an American citizen.
1908	Builds house in Plandome, Long Island, America.
1914	British film version of *Little Lord Fauntleroy*.
1917–18	Wins libel case, but slanged by press.
1918–24	Happy years, absorbed in writing, gardening and grandchildren.
1924–29	October: death of Burnett, aged nearly 75.

EDITH NESBIT (1858–1924)

1858	15 August: born at 58 Lower Kennington Lane, London, to John Nesbit, a teacher of agriculture and chemistry at his agricultural college, and Sarah, née Alderton, the youngest of five children. (One brother died before her birth; one sister is the offspring of her mother's first marriage.)
1862	Death of father, aged 43. Sarah Nesbit runs the agricultural college herself.
1866–71	Nesbit's sister Mary becomes consumptive. Sarah Nesbit searches for a cure abroad. Nesbit goes to / runs away from a series of much-loathed schools, between holidays in France with her family.
1867	Nesbit terrified by the mummies of Bordeaux that will reappear as the Ugli-Wuglies in *The Enchanted Castle*.
1871	Death of Mary. Sarah Nesbit moves her remaining family to Halstead Hall in her home county, Kent – Nesbit's adored childhood home.
1875	Loss of money. Nesbit family move to Islington.
1876	First known published verse, 'A Year Ago', in the magazine *Good Words*. Publishes poems fairly regularly during teen years; dreams of becoming great poet.
1877	Nesbit meets Hubert Bland, a very intelligent bank clerk. She breaks off engagement to another bank clerk.
1879	Nesbit moves to Blackheath, under the name Mrs Bland. Tells everyone she's married. Bland shares

his time between Nesbit and his mother and her companion, Maggie, pregnant with Bland's son. Bland's affair with Maggie lasts ten years.

1880   22 April: Nesbit marries Bland, now a brush manufacturer, in a London registry office; 22 June: birth of son, Paul.

1881   2 December: birth of daughter, Iris.

1884   Nesbit and Bland begin collaborating in writing novels; Bland begins career as a writer. Nesbit meets Shaw through the Fabian society – in love with him for about three years.

1885   8 January: birth of son, Fabian, named after the Fabian society.

1886   Move to bigger house in Dorville Road, Blackheath. Alice Hoatson moves in with them, pregnant with Bland's child. Nesbit gives birth to stillborn child. Alice gives birth to Rosamund Bland, adopted by Nesbit.

1886–1889   Publishes a plethora of pot-boiler children's stories, as well as adult novels and poetry.

1889   Moves to bigger house, Birch Grove.

1892   Meets Oswald Barron, who inspires her to find her voice, in enjoyment of recreating her own childhood and arousing sense of past.

1894   Moves to bigger house, Three Gables, Grove Park.

1896–7   Writes series of autobiographical articles on childhood for *Girl's Own Paper*.

1897   Publication of *The Treasure Seekers* in *Father Christmas*, a supplement to the *Illustrated London News*.

1898   Next six episodes of *The Treasure Seekers* published in the *Pall Mall Magazine*. Falls in love with and moves to Well Hall, where she lives for twenty years, writes her best books and gives memorable parties. Shortly after moving, Nesbit loses the baby she has been carrying.

1899   Publication of *The Treasure Seekers* as a book. Its tremendous popularity heralds the start of Nesbit's golden vein of writing. For the next eleven years she produces one or more resoundingly

	successful children's books per year, as well as a stream of less well known ones, adult novels and poetry. Alice gives birth to Bland's son, John, who, like Rosamund, is adopted by Nesbit.
1900	Death of Fabian after adenoids operation.
1902	Death of Nesbit's mother.
1902–6	Friendship with the Wellses, which comes to grief over the Fabian Society and H. G. Wells's unsuccessful elopement with Rosamund.
1914	Death of Hubert.
1917	Nesbit marries Thomas Tucker.
1921	Nesbit's money runs out; sells her beloved Well Hall; moves to brick-built huts, the 'Long Boat' and the 'Jolly Boat', near Dymchurch, Kent.
1924	4 May: death of Nesbit, aged 66.

1

Introduction: Threads in the Tapestry

Mrs Ewing, Mrs Molesworth, Frances Hodgson Burnett and E. Nesbit were the most popular children's authors of their day. Their books have come to symbolize to succeeding generations a convention, entrenched as firmly as folklore, in which childhood is as halcyon as society is stable. Yet they led extraordinary, unconventional lives. It seems that who the Victorians actually were, how they wished to be seen, and how they have come down to us, are very different things. An analysis of these four women and their works uncovers a rich variety of paradoxes. Their books never echo their own irregular lifestyles, but revere a family idyll, though they show happiness in Utopia is elusive. Their fictional families seethe with lonely, anxious individuals longing to fulfil themselves, aware that their first duty is owed not to self but to the family. The resulting struggle echoes the tug-of-war between duty and progress, the twin-headed Hydra of late-Victorian thinking. The texts continually test boundaries and examine norms. The strong Victorian hierarchical family looks increasingly like a fortress in a siege of unprecedented and rapid social change, defending searing doubts about religion, gender, class and work.

It is impossible fully to understand the ethos and impetus of an age without an understanding of the hopes, fears and expectations for its children. Mrs Ewing wrote her first work, *Melchior's Dream and Other Stories*, in 1862; E. Nesbit's last full-length children's book, *Wet Magic*, was published in 1913. This book will attempt to draw back the curtain a little on the beliefs and values of the Victorians and Edwardians during this period through the lives and literature of these four major contributors to the image of childhood.

1

THE CHILD IN THE TEXT

What do you suppose is the use of a child without any meaning?
(Lewis Carroll, *Through the Looking Glass and What Alice Found There*, 1872)

The late nineteenth and early twentieth centuries celebrated childhood as never before. Early nineteenth-century writers such as Wordsworth, Coleridge and Blake saw childhood as a state of simplicity, an exemplar in a world of adult blight. Out of this grew, as Dickens's works show, a consciousness of the frailty of childhood and of adult responsibility for the child in society. This image of childhood purity and fragility erupted into an Edwardian nostalgic yearning for its ephemeral perfection, peaking in Barrie's eternal boy, *Peter Pan* (1904). The late Victorian/Edwardian fanfare of childhood emerged from a melting pot, and expressed itself in a so-called golden age of children's literature.

But how did children's literature become attached to an adult, adulatory image of childhood? Why was childish inexperience granted a literary status of inner truth? Who was the archetypal Victorian/Edwardian child in contemporary books? From what parentage did he/she spring?

The answers begin in eighteenth-century Romanticism. The Romantic vision saw children as a distillation of an integrity lost to adults. Rousseau's assertion that a child was instinctively moral, corruptible only by an immoral society, was adopted wholeheartedly by the Romantics. The child became the fount and vessel of truth and wisdom.

> Within the Romantic discourse of essential childhood, the mind of the child is set up as a sanctuary or bank vault of valuable but socially-endangered psychological powers: idealism, holism, vision, animism, faith and isolated self-sufficiency. From these powers is derived the spiritual authority that made Wordsworth speak of the child as a 'seer blest' and De Quincey praise the child's 'special power of listening for the tones of truth.' It is through these powers of consciousness, that the solitary child becomes, especially in the writings of Coleridge and Wordsworth, both the symbolic representative of the creative mind and the repository of creative power to be reclaimed by the retrospective adult self.[1]

The 'seer' child overcame the rearguard early nineteenth-century moralists' view of the child as instrument of original sin. Mrs Sherwood, 'first in the field of pious slaughter',[2] as Charlotte M. Yonge, herself a close runner-up, described her a generation later, was the genre's arch-moralist. Inserted among entrancing detail of play, lessons, clothes, food, pets, interiors and gardens, Lucy, Emily and Henry's childish misdemeanours in the first volume of *The Fairchild Family* (1818) are exaggerated into serious sin. Mr and Mrs Fairchild worry more about eternity than present squalls, keeping hell at bay with Bible quotations and exemplary deaths. A sibling fight inspires Mr Fairchild to show his children the hanging remains of a murderer. Mrs Fairchild points out frequently[3] that children are born with wicked hearts. By 1847, in the final volume, the morbidity and gruesomeness disappear. Mrs Sherwood is 'quite sure...our heavenly Father...will lead us hereafter to glory'. By mid-century the mixture of secularism and Romanticism led not only to the 'seer' child in literature, but to the cheerful family tale.

The Romantic concept of the child was enhanced by a nineteenth-century interpretation of the Judaeo-Christian tradition. Moses, the baby in the bulrushes who became a prince and spiritual leader; the boy David who conquered the giant Goliath; little Samuel who heard God's voice; 12-year-old Jesus who trounced the rabbis with his searing questions, were all miraculous, visionary children, wiser than adults. Since, during the nineteenth century, church and Sunday School attendance were totems of duty and respectability, these Bible stories were entrenched in a national bourgeois consciousness, just as family prayers and learning Collects were norms of middle-class daily life. Paintings of biblical children such as *The Infant Samuel* and *The Infant Timothy* (James Sant, RA, 1820–1916), and *Peace, or a Little Child Shall Lead Them* (William Strutt, 1896) transformed their Semitic roots into an Anglo-Saxon flaxen beauty that echoed St Augustine's 'non Angli sed angeli' (not Angles, but angels). Reproductions hung in countless Victorian and Edwardian homes. Late Victorians saw the child as an icon of transcendence and superiority. Paint and print bottled this perception, imbibed by an eager audience.

Childhood, however, was defined by class. Upper-class children could linger in childhood while the poor were hardly children at all. In agricultural and industrial areas they were small wage-earning cogs in the system. In cities they were 'street arabs', seen not as individuals but as an alien, barbarous swarming blot on society. Their loss of innocence was assumed to be inevitable. Mayhew, the mid-century chronicler of the poor, found guttersnipes 'untaught, mistaught, maltreated, neglected', growing up learning 'unrestrained indulgence of the most corrupt appetites of our nature', their faces, he found, adult, sharp and corrupt.[4]

Only as child protection increased during the century did the poor child play an heroic role in children's books. The age of consent for a girl was 12 until 1875, 13 until 1885, when it was raised to 16 by the Criminal Law Amendment Act. The Factory Act of 1878 codified earlier attempts to limit children's hours of work; the Education Act of 1880 made elementary education compulsory until 13. The prolongation of working-class childhood gave it a middle-class emphasis in children's literature. It was now not unrealistic to isolate from the multitude a sympathetic waif who pined for religion, education and understanding.

In the early nineteenth century, children's writers were divided into two camps; the moralists, such as Maria Edgeworth, who believed in reason rather than emotion (Edgeworth's *The Purple Jar* is a typical story in which Rosamond asks for a deceptively pretty but useless purple jar rather than the new shoes she needs, and suffers consequently) and the Evangelicals who were passionately concerned to give everybody, rich and poor, the chance of eternity. Evangelical writers did not want to overturn the social structure, but promoted education and literacy, not as social reform, but as a path to God. Their books graphically describe the harrowing encounters of the child heroes/heroines with poverty and death; for instance, Maria Charlesworth's *Ministering Children* (1854), 'Brenda's' *Froggy's Little Brother* (1875), Hesba Stretton's *Jessica's First Prayer* (1867) and *Little Meg's Children* (1868), and Mrs O. F. Walton's *A Peep Behind the Scenes* (1877).

The plot of *A Peep Behind the Scenes* is a stirring example of the Evangelical approach to the child and the world. Little Rosalie lives in a caravan with Norah, her dying mother, and her cruel father. They travel with a circus, and her father produces plays in which Rosalie acts. Just before Norah dies, she begs Rosalie to find God, confessing her own guilt. She tells Rosalie that she had been born a lady, had eloped into the arms of the theatre, having rejected the religious pleas of her sister Lucy. Bitter experience has led her to acknowledge the false glamour behind the scenes. Rosalie's father snubs his child's religious leanings, forces Rosalie to perform on the stage while her mother draws her last breath, marries a woman who proves a cruel stepmother, and soon rolls under the wheels of a van, senseless with drink. Rosalie agonises not for her orphan state but for her father's afterlife ('Oh, where was he now? Was his soul safe?'), while the text condemns him to eternal damnation. He had scorned God's 'voice of love and now it was too late'.[5] Rosalie's stepmother threatens her with the workhouse, but Rosalie runs away to find her aunt Lucy, now a clergyman's wife. Rosalie is adopted and lives happily ever after. She feels she has come home to the Green Pastures of the Psalm, sustained by the love of the Good Shepherd. On the way, she has converted Mother Minikin, a circus dwarf, Toby, her father's handyman, Betsey Ann, her stepmother's kitchen-maid, and Jessie, a teenager who tried to run away to join the circus. Walton's portrayal of Rosalie's unhappiness, tenacity, and sense of self-worth is a vivid, memorable mixture of sentimentality and realism. The child in Victorian/Edwardian texts, who appears as a strong individual, bursting with feeling, triumphing over adversity, a force for good, is the offspring of the Evangelicals as well as the Romantics.

While poor children starred in children's literature only if they were very good, the rich could be endearingly bad. Prancing into print in 1839 were the first naughty-but-nice upper-class children. Their creator, Catherine Sinclair, in her preface to *Holiday House* dismissed current children's books, 'a mere record of dry facts, unenlivened with any appeal to the heart, or any excitement to the fancy', and aimed to write the opposite, turning upside down perceived gender ideals. Young Harry sets the house on fire – an embryonic pater familias attempts to ruin the family seat. Little Laura destroys all her frocks, the outward declaration of pretty femininity. Their behaviour, Sinclair insists, is easily forgivable since it springs from merry, youthful hearts. They are finally bridled as they

5

attend their saintly elder brother's lengthy deathbed, a scene that omits no sobering detail, not even his final outburst of fatal spots.

Sinclair introduced into children's literature the subversive notion that a healthy process from childhood freedom to adult responsibility may include wildness and disobedience, a popular theme in the Victorian domestic children's tale, taken to extreme lengths in Flora Shaw's *Castle Blair* (1878). Here a family of upper-class Irish children vacillate between savagery and sentiment. Murtagh, aged about 12, becomes involved with the Irish Revolutionary Movement, and arranges the murder of a land agent who he believes oppresses the tenants. A conscience-crisis stops him just in time. Murtagh's character surges with loyalty and valour, an example of the tradition of manly boy-heroes of books of the latter half of the nineteenth century. The earlier heroic image of the Byronic man of sensibility developed into a bold, patriotic definition of masculinity that fed the cult of the intrepid Empire-builder and the invincible patriarch of the home.

The authors of this genre, such as Robert Ballantyne (1825–94), G. A. Henty (1839–1902), Talbot Baines Reed (1852–93), H. Rider Haggard (1856–1925) and Rudyard Kipling (1865–1936), wrote about boys for boys. Victorian gender stereotyping meant that male writers wrote action-packed school and adventure stories, and female writers, such as Jean Ingelow (1820-1897), Elizabeth Hart (1822–c.1890), Charlotte M. Yonge (1823–1901), Mrs Craik (1826–87), Hesba Stretton (1832–1911), Alice Corkran (1850–1916), and L. T. Meade (1854–1914), wrote girls' stories that dwelt on domesticity and feelings. Reynolds suggests that the demand by girls for more exciting literature led to the development of books aimed at both boys and girls. The result was the Victorian family story, the domain of Mrs Ewing, Mrs Molesworth, Frances Hodgson Burnet and E. Nesbit.

> Such books replace the ethos of confidence, mastery, and independence based on masculine superiority with one based on class. In them, sex roles are unambiguous, and accordingly the adventures have been domesticated, (so as to rule out potentially compromising situations for the female characters and readers): the emphasis is on celebrating family life rather than on conquering foreign lands and exotic peoples.[6]

The Victorian age was one of social fluidity. The speed of change in politics, education and philosophy created see-saw effects in social expectations and standards. New industrial fortunes flourished; ancient money disappeared through dissipation and economic disasters. Everyone, however, wanted a safe place on the class bandwagon. As Froude, the nineteenth century historian, explains: 'To push on, to climb vigorously on the slippery slopes of the social ladder, to raise ourselves out of the rank of life in which we were born, is now converted into a duty.'[7] Class was a Victorian obsession that dominated the minutiae of life and fiction.

The directives of hierarchy were linked to behaviour, shrouded by a code of discretion. Judgements were frequently described in French – *noblesse oblige, nouveau riche, arriviste, parvenu, comme il faut* – reflecting a Victorian stance of oblique frankness, comprehensible only to those who understood its nuances. Blatant transgressors of the rules were ostracized, and irregularities concealed. 'Never comment on a likeness', 'Curiosity killed the cat', were common Victorian expressions. Burnett in her autobiography of childhood describes how early she understood the tacit class–morality link. To her childish 'simple, gentle mind', the words 'lady' and 'gentlemen' meant 'something very upright and fine'.

> To be unkindly and selfish was not only base but somehow vulgar too – and...the people who were not born in the 'back streets' naturally avoided these things as they avoided dropping their h's and speaking the dialect.[8]

Burnett's life, like Molesworth's and Nesbit's, was rife with irregularities, though not a hint of them appeared in their children's books. There they celebrated duty, convention, moral superiority, and self-help; silent passwords, despite the ambiguities they entailed, to the betterment and safety that all middle-class parents wanted for their children.

For the Victorians were past masters of the paradox. Religious doubt, for instance, inspired by Darwinian theories, marched with the overwhelming religious structure of middle-class Britain. Mostly, those who doubted kept quiet, in order to avoid ostracism, and to support family and social stability. The morality demanded by Christianity was at odds with the competition and self-interest of the new commercial age. In order to survive it, Thackeray ironically advised, 'If your neighbour's foot obstructs you, stamp on it.'[9] Industrialization led to inequality of wealth and health, while the countryside was treasured as it was destroyed. Darwin's thesis, popularly understood to describe the fall of the weak, contradicted movements to help the weakest, such as prison reform, the Married Women's Property Act, and Factory and Education Acts. An unparalleled age of speed and technological change gave a sense of excitement and restlessness, side by side with a craving for stability. Ideals of sexual purity created double standards in both gender and class. The Victorians allowed the macho, Lothario male experiences forbidden to the virginal 'angel of the house', shielded in her armour of laces, buttons, and layers of petticoats, her figure hidden by corset and bustle. Lower-class women, less clad, were considered more coarse and available then their upper-class sisters. Women's best hope of status and security lay in marriage, yet the urgency of their pursuit required subtlety. Bad women were bold, and good women were unobtrusive. Girls had to attract men without appearing to do so.

Perhaps in response to a way of life that hid feelings behind façades, a new fantasy genre of children's literature emerged. While early Victorians moralists censored fairy stories as wicked lies, the end of the century revered them 'practically as engines for the propulsion of all the virtues into the little mind'.[10] The change took place mid-century, with an unprecedented outpouring of magic tales: new translations from the Grimm brothers between 1839 and 1855, Lear's *A Book of Nonsense* (1846), the translation of Hans Christian Andersen's *Wonderful Stories for Children* (1846), Ruskin's *King of the Golden River* (1851), Thackeray's *The Rose and the Ring* (1855), Charles Kingsley's *The Water Babies* (1863), George MacDonald's *The Light Princess* (1864), Lewis Carroll's *Alice in Wonderland* (1865), and Frances Browne's *Granny's Wonderful Chair* (1856). Carpenter points out that Kingsley, Carroll and MacDonald all began writing their children's stories within weeks of each other. All were ministers of religion who eschewed conventional religious teaching in their children's stories.

Though fantasy-escapes have always been normal outlets of the human psyche, their mid-century popularity echoes an unspoken disquiet with religion, politics, morals and mores, while they also reflect the Victorian masking/revealing frame of mind, since fantasy both blocks and exposes realism. The innovative mid-century writers, and others such as Mary de Morgan and Christina Rossetti, explored gender equality and the importance of the creative spirit, searching beyond society, into self and nature, to gain divine insight, suggesting alternative ways of conduct. The fairy tale became a holdall for a collection of nineteenth-century concerns.

Ewing, Molesworth, Burnett and Nesbit followed the pattern set by their predecessors in investigating establishment pillars – in their own unique ways. Ewing, whose mother admired and encouraged Carroll, swung like him away from religion. Although Ewing had a weakness for pathos, she liked jollity too. Her poem 'The Burial of the Linnet' cast her happily back to her own vicarage childhood memories burying dead pets; it gave children an example of robust imitative play in a period in which many would have experienced the death of a parent or sibling; it parodies the pomp of Victorian mourning ceremonies.

> Found in the garden – dead in his beauty.
> Ah! that a linnet should die in the spring!
> Bury him, comrades, in pitiful duty,
> Muffle the dinner-bell, solemnly ring...

Her spoof of the solemn epithets of mourning, a ritual stiff with etiquette that bolstered middle-class respectability, echoes Carroll's reworkings of Watt's *Divine and Moral Songs* (1715 and still in wide circulation in the nineteenth century). Watt's poem is a rallying cry to duty, productivity and hard work, handrails to the exit from the working class: 'How doth the busy little bee/ Improve each shining hour/ And gather honey all the day/ From every opening flower!' Carroll translates it into nonsense in *Alice in Wonderland*: 'How doth the little crocodile/ Improve his shining tail/ And pour the waters of the Nile/ On every golden scale!'

Carroll's parodies opened doors. Compare Carroll's *Wonderland* mockery of courtly ritual through his monstrous queens with Molesworth's similar derision of hierarchy and etiquette in her fairy story *The Reel Fairies* (1875). Here lonely little Louisa dreams she becomes queen of the cotton reels in her mother's workbasket, magically transformed into subjects. Stiff and tired sitting on the throne, she wants to get off. 'Her majesty wishes to take a little exercise,' buzz the cotton reels, jerking the throne and holding her fast to it. She struggles. They jerk her more violently – 'Her majesty wishes to take a little *more* exercise' – while imprisoning her feet on her footstool. Sewing, a Victorian symbol of femininity, embodies stillness and domesticity. In this story, Louisa is trapped by sewing appurtenances. Her nightmare does not herald the Victorian miss realizing the folly of wishing for grandeur. Instead her mother is inspired to make new resolutions. She realizes she has neglected Louisa, having glimpsed 'that strange, fantastic, mysterious world, which we call a child's imagination'. All Molesworth's children's books are a testament to her conviction that children are the result of their upbringing and that parents must realize their responsibilities.

Carroll's legacy was twofold. He introduced amorality into children's literature – 'liberty of thought', as Harvey Darton pointed out. 'Henceforth fear had gone.'[11] Carroll told a friend his books 'have no religious teaching in them whatever – in fact they do not teach anything at all'.[12] His Romantic vision of childhood as a nostalgic, wise, golden, finite time was continued by Burnett and Nesbit into the next century. He defines his vision in his preface poem in *Alice Through the Looking Glass* (1871), addressed to his child muse, Alice Liddell.

> Child of the pure unclouded brow
> And dreaming eyes of wonder
> Though time be fleet, and I and thou
> Are half a life asunder
>
> ...
>
> And though the shadow of a sigh
> May tremble through the story
> For 'happy summer days' gone by,
> And vanish'd summer glory –
> It shall not touch with breath of bale
> The pleasance of our fairy tale.

Though the *Alice* books are based on mathematics, logic and a tradition of Nonsense, nevertheless Molesworth's understanding of a child's imagination – 'strange, fantastic, mysterious' – Burnett's translation of childhood into distillations of beauty and perfection, and Nesbit's equation of childhood with freedom and bliss as she sighs for its passing, are a development of Alice's childish integrity pitted against adult topsy-turveydom.

Carroll showed the manuscript of *Alice in Wonderland* to his friend George MacDonald, who strongly approved it. MacDonald's own fairy tales, unlike Carroll's, were drenched in morals. MacDonald's obituary dubbed him 'the ancestor of imaginary writing for children informing a deep moral purpose, surrounding the powder with jam'.[13] Both Carroll and Macdonald created imaginary worlds with immutable, inexorable laws, an idea taken up enthusiastically by Ewing, Molesworth, Burnett and Nesbit. These four women rejected Carroll's amorality for Macdonald's moral mantle. Molesworth stated clearly that children's writers should create a playground, while 'never losing sight of what is *good* for them'.[14] Nesbit's children, exemplars of honour, glory in freedom and fun; 'perfect little trumps', as Andrew Lang described them.

MacDonald's fantasy lands pose possibilities of awesome things unknown. As Carpenter notes, he creates 'an alternative religious landscape which a child's mind could explore and which could offer spiritual nourishment'. *At the Back of the North Wind* takes its hero, Diamond, to a country where 'nothing went wrong neither was anything quite right. Only everything was going to be right some day.' Here Diamond finds 'something better than mere happiness'. Molesworth in *The Cuckoo Clock* created a land on the other side of the moon with a startling resemblance to the back of the North Wind, where everything was strange and silent, without light or time, leaving the heroine, Griselda, with a sense of wonderment. Similarly Nesbit's *The Enchanted Castle* ends with magic in which 'space is not, time is not…this instant is…a moment, and it is eternity'. Burnett's *The Secret Garden* revolves around a healing magic that comes from nature, and summons up telepathy and voices from the dead. Macdonald opened the door to a mystic yearning in children's literature for alternative spiritual fulfilment.

Diamond, as peerless and poetic as his name, is a throwback, like Alice and Kingsley's Tom in *The Water Babies*, to the eighteenth-century 'seer' child-innocent in a nineteenth-century scenario of adult disillusion and utopian dreams. This vehicle of innocence lived on in the works of Ewing, Molesworth, Burnett and Nesbit, pepped up with a dose of unease as they also used children's literature as a mouthpiece for a critical voice.

11

THE WOMAN WITH THE PEN

What a mercy you were married a good many years ago! You could hardly have succeeded in finding a wife now who had not published a Book or contributed to a Journal, or at least had a manuscript in progress!

(Jane Carlyle to Major David Davidson, 14 February 1859)[15]

Ewing, Molesworth, Burnet and Nesbit were as famous for their fantasy as for their family stories. Late-Victorian female writers produced children's fantasy stories in droves; writers include Mrs Craik, Mary De Morgan, Frances Browne and Christina Rossetti. The questions: Why did Victorian women write such successful children's fantasies? Why did their fantasies contain enduring resonances? are directly linked to larger questions: Why did women write so readily ? Why did nineteenth-century women become successful children's writers? The answers unfold in the way Victorians thought about women, and in the restrictive codes of the Victorian female work ethic. This was a labyrinth riddled with convention. Its structure prevented female emancipation. Only the medium of the pen gave speech to the female voice, though, as Mitchell points out, 'either financial necessity or high moral purpose were virtually prerequisites: the desire for self-expression, or success, or fame, or public influence was not consonant with true womanhood'.[16]

Although in the eighteenth century, middle-class women worked as plumbers, butchers, saddlers, the nineteenth century dubbed such employment both lower-class and unfeminine. Work for middle-class women was a maze of contradictions in which noblesse oblige, talent, self-denial, ambition, penury and femininity tugged in opposite directions. Ruskin had crystallized, in *Of Queen's Gardens*, the definitive label of femininity; women were 'wise and faithful counsellors', whose mission was to guard the shrine of home.[17] The 'angel in the house', as everyone knew, ought to be nurturing, pure, virtuous, and so selfless that, as Virginia Woolf said, 'if there was a draught, she sat in it'.[18] The sum of female perfection was summed up in Charles Kingsley's adage of Victorian upbringing: 'Be good, sweet maid, and let who will be clever.' Clever women were too mannish.

12

The 1851 census showed a surplus of women; this and economic booms and busts made work for some middle-class women a necessity. However, while the extent of female employment widened, its range narrowed. Women might follow professions that involved caring and creativity, like teaching, typing, nursing, dressmaking, millinery, painting (in 1850, Eliza Cook's Journal confirmed 'a woman may be an artist and a lady') – though they risked their respectability. Even the independent-minded writer Mrs Craik wrote of 'the not unnatural repugnance that is felt to woman's drawing from 'the life', attending anatomical discussions'.[19]

Women who went out to work lost home's protective aura. Beyond it lay the brutish connotations of the market place, the acknowledged hub of roughness and masculinity. Most families protected their girls, certain a woman's real place was in the home. Florence Nightingale, who loathed her family's relentless tentacles, and Josephine Butler, who risked her femininity in repealing the Contagious Diseases Acts, were unusual. As late as 1891, the middle-class girls' journal *The Girl's Home Companion* advised its readers, 'Lavish upon your home affection, attention, unselfishness, and banish from it all craving for excitement.' Women who tried to earn from home found a paucity of opportunity and reward. *The Girl's Own Paper* (1896) proposed only embroidery, knitting, copying, and plain perseverance, warning of poor pay.

But the woman who could write was fortunate and fulfilled. She could work from home, reaffirming its sanctuary while creating a bolt-hole from it. As Mrs Gaskell said, 'I am sure it is healthy for [women] to have the refuge of the hidden world of Art to shelter themselves in when too much pressed upon by daily small Lilliputian arrows of peddling cares.'[20] Women writers of novels and children's tales used their books subtly to declare their disquiet. In the same way that a mid-century explosion of fantasy was a coded commentary on unease, so a simultaneous deluge of female writers was evidence of their concerns that appeared, overt and hidden in their texts.

Writing was a legitimate gap in the strictures and structures of the feminine code through which the pent-up torrent could pour, as well as the only way to compete with men on a slightly more level playing field. In her writing, a woman's mental

13

powers were respected as much as possible for her time. Her femininity, provided she was married, remained unsullied. Married female authors were considered more womanly than single women. John Ludlow, reviewing Mrs Gaskell's *Ruth* in the *North British Review* compared Mrs Gaskell's 'full, wholesome, and most womanly perfection' with Miss Brontë, whom he found 'harsh, rough, unsatisfying, unwomanly'.[21] As Miller points out, 'Jane Eyre was reviled by contemporary reviewers. Elizabeth Rigby in the *Quarterly Review* (1848) concluded that if the book had been written by a woman, it was one who had "long forfeited the society of her own sex". The implication was that the author was a fallen woman who, through sexual indiscretion, had caused herself to be ostracised by respectable ladies.'[22] Female passion was, to the Victorians, at worst a short step from madness, at best rather vulgar and better shrouded. Most blameless of all, of course, were women who avoided adult passion in print altogether. But this does not wholly explain why the majority of Victorian children's books were written by women.

' "Books for children" – the press groans with their multitude,' said Charlotte M. Yonge.[23] The increase of women writers coincided with a surge of children's story books; a new phenomenon, even a cause for concern. 'Do [children's books] not rather, from their very numbers and attractiveness, do harm, by inducing children to confine their reading entirely to them?' asked a critic and educationalist in1897.[24] During the 1840s and 1850s, the book trade had responded to increased literacy and a growing middle class with a mass of adult publications. This introduced a new area of debate and definition: the social role of the writer. Poovey argues convincingly that male authors like Dickens thus created 'the textual construction of an individualist psychology'.

> This process was part of the legitimating and depoliticization of capitalist market and class relations...that the definition (and defence) of the English writer's social role was intimately involved in both and that stabilizing and mobilizing a particular image of woman, the domestic sphere, and woman's work were critical to all three.[25]

The social role of the Victorian female children's writer was equally innovative, as it undermined male assertions. Since writing was also an acknowledged female outlet, since children and domesticity was an exclusive female sphere, the writing of children's books was viewed as a commendable female occupation. Women writers, armed with an established creed of literary individualism, set about creating their own definitions of individualism in children's books, as they explored ethics, gender, religion and class under the feminine umbrella of upbringing. To the Victorians, women and children held the same status; both were considered pure and vulnerable; both were disenfranchised; both were legally disadvantaged. At the same time, child-power was stepping up. The birth rate dropped, allowing middle-class parents more money to spend on a mass of child-centred artefacts that flooded the market. The Victorian ambition of betterment, and its belief that instruction ranked alongside amusement, called for children's books, while technical advances lowered printing costs to provide plenty. Toys grew more splendid. Life-sized dolls, rocking-horses, toy theatres, mechanical toys, jigsaws, Noah's Arks, well-equipped dolls' houses occupied the best nurseries. Children's clothes, richly frilled, with falls of lace; children's education; children's equipment, like perambulators, parasols and twenty-bore guns, showed off their parent's wealth. Children's magazines were launched. Theatres produced children's plays 'for children and grown-*up* children', as the billboard for Burnett's play *The Little Princess* proclaimed. Illustrations of pretty children featured in advertisements. Their mixture of purity and potency was a winning seller. Children were not only a beacon of integrity but a powerful economic force in a society aiming ever upwards. As the Angel of the House grew into the New Woman, it is not surprising that women writers found themselves unconsciously annexing the power of the child in their bid for individualization, and as a vehicle for a voice.

The writers themselves were fully aware of the importance of their field, even if children's books were looked on, as Molesworth was told, as a 'small thing'. Molesworth posits her authorial impact with an annexation of the child's stance.

> If the responsibility of writing any book is grave, surely the gravest of all is that of writing for children? The whole position is strangely complicated, much more so than outsiders imagine. You have to be yourself, with your experience, your knowledge of good, and alas! of

15

evil too; and at the same time you must be the child, or at least in the child's place, and that, again, without any apparent stepping down.[26]

Briggs unpacks the effect of Nesbit's scheme in *The Story of the Treasure Seekers* of making Oswald the narrator/hero.

The device of adopting Oswald as narrator avoids the situation of the adult talking down to children. The further device of Oswald's inconsistent but often aspiringly literary third-person narrative also sets him up as a target for comic irony, the complacent Victorian patriarch in embryo. E. Nesbit can thus laugh with him and at him, enjoying his child's angle on the adult world while providing a subtle critique of his comfortable male assumptions.[27]

In her forward to her autobiography, Nesbit declared

When I was a little child I used to pray fervently, tearfully, that when I should be grown up I might never forget what I thought and felt and suffered then. Let these pages speak for me, and bear witness that I have not forgotten.[28]

Her fictional children, like those of Ewing, Molesworth and Burnett, are the sum of the past with a new slant added. The eighteenth-century seer, the Evangelical sinner, the romp, and the sensitive, redeeming waif drenched in sentimentality, were given a dose of realism, produced by the writer identifying with the child, and legitimating the child's thought process. This realism underpinned a new questioning of adult values from the freshness of a child's viewpoint, while outwardly supporting them. These four writers explored female individualism, using codes that were convoluted yet clear, like the corkscrew conventions of the female work ethic, itself based on an unreal, iconic vision of a woman, and her real need of fulfilment. Such subversive steps were possible behind the safety curtain of the family.

This quartet all wrote stories and fantasies based on the family experience. They were themselves family-based. Their backgrounds of marriage and family illuminated their status as children's writers, giving their books a special resonance of experience and respectability. Juliana Ewing and Louisa Molesworth, under the soubriquet of 'Mrs', became literary bastions of childhood. Frances Hodgson Burnett was known to have based her most famous character, Little Lord Fauntleroy, on her own son. Edith Bland, though she chose the androgynous nom-de-plume of E. Nesbit, eventually presented a rumbustious family front of five children, a large country house and devoted husband. All four, however, had either unsatisfactory or disastrous marriages. The fact that, for three out of the four, respectability was a sham was a well-kept secret.

2

Juliana Horatia Ewing

I have lived in sunshine all my life.

(Letter to Mrs Gatty, 23 August 1868)

Of the four subjects of this study, Ewing was the least rebellious, the most dutiful, the most self-effacing, with the kindest, happiest nature. A range of sources, including her private letters and diaries and contemporary reviews, paint a picture of a woman who was non-grasping, non-pushy, quietly uncomplaining always. She shines as an example of a *lady*, the epitome of mid-nineteenth-century female perfection. Her character and the mores of her time fitted each other like a well-cut glove, so that a biographical exploration of her life and works acts not only as an insight into the far-off visions of a vanished age, but also the reason why her books form no part of the present classical canon of children's literature. Of the four, she is the most forgotten. Nothing of her work remains in print for children, though she has always had her adult critical fans. 'Her works are likely to appeal to the sort of child who will, when grown-up, appreciate Jane Austen. If children today fail to find [validity in her values] the fault is not with Mrs Ewing.'[1] Ewing was fatally representative of the Victorian fragile female image. She was as frail as she was good, and died aged 44. In true Victorian style of secrets behind closed doors, the exact nature of her last disease was never revealed. Perhaps it was never fully known. Throughout her life her ill health was variously and vaguely diagnosed, and though she had the best opinions, including Queen Victoria's doctor, medical knowledge could not help her.

JERUSALEM THE GOLDEN

There was of course more to Juliana Ewing than a cardboard stereotype of revered Victorian womanhood. Beneath this mantle, she was spirited, bossy and courageous, characteristics inherited from her immediate forebears. Her maternal grandfather was Alexander Scott (1768–1840) a remarkable linguist, heroically adventurous, and chaplain to Nelson. Scott served on board the *Victory* at Trafalger, and held the dying admiral in his arms. He left such momentous experiences to become an obscure country clergyman, so poor that the parents of the girl he fell in love with, Mary Ryder, refused to let them marry. Undaunted, they eloped. Four years later, Mary died, leaving two daughters, Horatia and Margaret.

Margaret grew up to be an unusual woman. Enthusiastic, strong-minded, hating to be idle, gripped by, among other passions, seaweeds and sundials, she radiated warmth and a formidable intellect. She married a clergyman, Alfred Gatty, who was given by Margaret's Ryder uncle the living of Ecclesfield in Cheshire. The Gattys had ten children, eight of whom survived, the second of whom was Juliana Horatia, named after Nelson, and known to her family as Julie. There was never enough money and Mrs Gatty, to eke out the budget, seized upon writing. She produced highly esteemed children's stories, contributed to Charlotte M. Yonge's magazine, the *Monthly Packet*, and edited the children's journal, *Aunt Judy's Magazine*, which ran for twenty years from 1866, though, due to the vagaries of publishing, only in one year did it ever make a profit. The magazine was the most famous of its period. Mrs Gatty lured notable contributors such as Hans Christian Andersen and Lewis Carroll. She was full of confident, bossy encouragement. On publishing Carroll's *Bruno's Revenge* in *Aunt Judy's Magazine* in 1867, she told him

> I am so *proud* for Aunt Judy that you have honoured her by sending it here rather than to the *Cornhill* or one of the grander magazines. One word more. Make this one of a series. You may have great mathematical abilities, but so have hundreds of others. This talent is peculiarly your own, and as an Englishman you are almost unique.[2]

19

Carroll's sequal, *Sylvie and Bruno* appeared in 1893, well after the demise of the magazine. He acknowledged in his preface its origin from a tale written at Mrs Gatty's request.

She also wrote *British Seaweeds* (1872), a standard work, and had the distinction of having a seaweed and a sea worm named after her. (*Gattya pinella* and *Gattia spectabilis*) She encouraged Ewing to write, recognizing her talent. Living with Margaret, her husband said, was 'a liberal education'.[3]

Ewing was deeply influenced by her mother. To appreciate Mrs Gatty is to understand Ewing. Mrs Gatty was original but also hidebound. Recommending suitable clothes for seaweed hunting in a period that equated female indecency with a flash of leg, she urged women to 'lay aside all thought of conventional appearances' and wear above-ankle petticoats.[4] Conversely she was appalled by the feminist Frances Power Cobbe. 'To hear a woman hold forth in public, except when she is acting and not supposed to be herself, is like listening to bells rung backwards.'[5] Mrs Gatty's books reveal her precepts of upbringing. In 'Out of the Way' in *Aunt Judy's Tales*, for instance, the youngest child is tiresomely apparent while the family is packing for a holiday. At last he disappears under a table. His new unobtrusiveness becomes a moral about 'the modesty which arises out of that humility of spirit which "vaunteth not itself"',[6] and he is praised at last.

The Gatty family absorbed this self-effacement lesson faithfully. Ewing's story *The Brownies* (1865), thirty years after her death, inspired Baden-Powell to create the junior branch of the Girl Guide movement in 1915, copying its name, ethos and rituals. Her sisters, who controlled the copyright, never sought acknowledgement. Ewing herself was always modest. In 1871 she told Mr Bell, who published all Gatty and Ewing work, 'Children's literature...will probably be my forte – if I ever reach success at all.' By this time she had written two successful children's books and a glut of popular magazine stories. Her relationship with Mr Bell reveals a loyalty and lack of ruthlessness that did nothing to help her financially. Though exasperated by his inefficiency – 'You can't conceive of old Bell's muddle and obstinacy,' she exploded to her husband in 1879 – she stayed with him. Ewing, in common with other authors, paid for the printing and binding of her books, then sold them on to Bell, who priced and distributed them, giving her a profit. This was always small, but Ewing never raised her voice: 'Please be sure *I* shall be pleased with whatever you arrange' (1872). She prodded him, but gently. A typical comment: 'Don't think me fidgety, but does it not seem a pity to miss Easter tide when people often make presents to children' (1872). 'I don't want to be grasping'(1868) – this was in respect of a profit-share from translation. Appalled at his suggestion that her 'valueless phiz' should appear as a frontispiece: 'I hate refusing you anything, but I *couldn't* stand it' (1878). 'I am not a name, I am no poet,' she told him. Flamboyance and chutzpah, tools of the trade to Burnett and Nesbit, were anathema to Ewing's nature and nurture.

Ewing, 'a refined little teapot'[7] as her mother described her babyhood manner, was nicknamed 'Aunt Judy' by her family since from early childhood she took on an aunt-like mantle of benevolence. Small and slight with straight fair hair, and thin, firm features, she set a good example and kept her siblings amused with stories and 'projukes' as they called her games. She had a lilac bush in the garden, 'Julie's Bower', fronted with planks laid on upended flower pots. Here the little ones sat listening to her tales. One sister, called Dot by her family and Fatty by Ewing, said she tyrannized them, adding that they all so enjoyed it that they allowed her full sway. In her early 20s, she gave a third of the money she made by writing to charity, and spent leftovers on holidays for sickly family members, though she was frequently unwell herself. Her father used to tease her saying 'Dear Juliana is always *better thank you* but never *quite well'*, which reveals the silent front she put on her ill health.[8]

Her childhood nickname showed prescience. Ewing was destined always to be an aunt but never a mother. Her siblings produced quantities of children, Ewing none. As Aunt Judy, however, she inspired the titles of her mother's work (*Aunt Judy's Tales* (1859), *Aunt Judy's Letters* (1862), *Aunt Judy's Magazine*, 1866–88). Everyone, even Ruskin, who became a friend, called her Aunt Judy. The 'Victorian auntly narrative voice' has been defined as a literary device of talking down to children, thus awakening the child reader's sense of informality and creative involvement in story-telling.[9] Ewing's voice differed. She wanted to lure her readers alongside as she raised them upwards. Her books were like her childhood stories for her siblings in which, her mother said, 'with so much drollery and amusement, there was sure to be mixed up some odd scraps of information, or bits of good advice'.[10] Mrs Gatty's praise contains the staple ingredients of approved Victorian child-rearing: amusement laced with moral instruction. Ewing added her own angle to this mixture: a new irony and sympathetic understanding of the child. Her sometimes intricate style earned her criticism. Molesworth admitted contemporary critics thought Ewing's books were 'more about than for children sometimes 'beyond' an average child's full comprehension', though she believed Ewing's mental leaps made children think.[11]

Mrs Gatty, firm upholder of her generation's gender discrimination in education, taught her daughters herself with an occasional governess, pleased that they drudged in the parish 'like unpaid curates'. The four boys went to the best public schools: Eton, Winchester, Marlborough and Charterhouse. All the children were talented and industrious. Ewing edited a family magazine, an original, sophisticated production of articles, stories, poems, correspondence and songs. Gatty family life was busy, and fun; wholesome but not goody-goody, as Ewing's diary entries show. Writing poetry with her sisters induced laughter 'till I made my head ache' (28 February 1856). There were fights: 'Regie threw a roasted apple at my head' (9 April 1856); teasing: 'we gammoned Madge by bringing her a little bit of D[ot]'s hair pretending it was Captain Burgh's whom we had seen having his hair cut – so we said' (11 April 1856), and comforting: 'Regie going to school. Went to his room while he was dressing. He was crying and in a dreadful state. Drove with him to Sheffield by his request and told him the end of the story on the way' (10 September1856). On Ewing's seventeenth birthday: 'Rode up to the workhouse to ask the children down to tea out of doors. They came. Games etc. tea under the oak' (3 August 1858). Dotted around the vicarage were prestigious relics such as Nelson's chair, but the house was frugal, lacking dining room curtains and plentiful coal. In winter they shivered. 'Dressed and said my prayers between the kitchen and the dining room as I got frozen,' Ewing noted, aged 20.

They all adored home. In a confession game in which players were asked, 'In what place would you most like to live?' all claimed Ecclesfield. Lovingly, they reproduced the vicarage, church and rambling countryside in their sketchbooks. Grown-up and scattered, in letters, in visits, they longed for the rarefied, enchanted air of home. Ewing, aged 26, in her first year of marriage, writing to her mother from Canada, was wrung with homesickness.

'Ecclesfield' just rushed over me so unbearably that I *couldn't* hold out...I broke down & had 'a regular good cry.' – I know it was very selfish, for *he* [her husband] thinks me quite Home enough...and I fully expected him to be vexed – though keep it back I couldn't.[12]

Home was apparently an idyll that seemed to touch all who knew it. Ewing's niece, when introduced to people who had known the Gatty family, was aware of 'a sudden hopeful glance, as if I could create for them a magic that was dead'.[13] Ewing tried in her life and works to recreate the robust salubrity of her home that she believed was best for moral fibre and family life.

By 1861, when Juliana was 20, she was contributing regularly to Charlotte M. Yonge's *Monthly Packet* magazine. Yonge, by now established as England's expert on children's literature, admired the 'poetry' of Mrs Gatty's work and the delicacy of Juliana's. That year Yonge came to stay at Ecclesfield. Juliana, who practised observations in her diary, noted, 'Would be beautiful but for a something. A want partly of happiness, partly of appreciativeness, partly of *calm* about her.' The Ecclesfield summing up of Yonge's nature – 'nervous and excitable, speaking *shrilly*', disapproved Mrs Gatty – was the opposite of Juliana's own outward air of serenity, just as Yonge's example of spinsterhood would have made her miserable. Ewing craved affection, declaring, 'few people are weaker than I as regards the luxury of being loved'.[14]

Love came when she was 25. Alexander Ewing, known as Rex, was a family friend, a soldier and musician. He had composed the tune of 'Jerusalem the Golden', which had become an integral part of the church service. Dame Ethel Smyth, the composer, who first met him aged 12, found in his famous tune 'a sort of groping ecstasy'. Juliana was smitten, though her parents were not. Rex had little money and poor prospects, though he measured up on other counts, being high church and a gentleman, closely related to a bishop. He began writing almost daily; Juliana's diary, interspersed with her usual entry, 'feeling seedy', now included, 'heard from my Boy...witty letter...jolly letter...darling letter'. When he stayed, she confided to her diary, they 'flapdoodlised rather'. The Gatty parents told her to stop his letters. Juliana 'tried to find an opportunity to tell AE about not writing. Couldn't somehow...' When she did, Rex, 'very low', banged on the piano. At last after 'awful rows' with her parents and the offer of an army posting in Frederickton, Canada, that upped Rex's pay, the Gattys relented. Juliana, her mother conceded, was 'brilliantly happy', but 'we shall have a terrible loss.' They married 1867.

Ewing was in clover. 'He suits me to a shade.' Straight after the wedding they set sail for Canada, Rex ecstatic at carrying her off. A year later he triumphantly addressed his mother-in-law, 'You know her, (you suppose) pretty well – very well; but – as a daughter. It has been given to me to know her as a wife.'[15] The Gattys hated to think of their beloved, frail daughter enduring the horrors of the long sea-voyage, let alone the rigours of foreign climes. Mrs Gatty sent endless anxious letters. Ewing was patience itself. 'There are bitter days when the wind takes your breath and freezes your nose and fingers', but then she simply stayed indoors. [16] 'Pray don't worry your dear self about the heat. It never lasts long. I assure you I thoroughly enjoy the climate as a whole – winter – summer – spring & autumn.'[17] 'As to the fatigue of walking on snowshoes – I don't think it fatiguing – it is charming...it is an amusement like skating'.[18]

She always hid grim truth from others until she had dealt with it. She never let on about her cold house until describing the 'Paradise of warmth' when they moved. The very thought of marriage had scared her stiff 'which used to put Rex into a rage then as he could never understand it', she told her sister a year later, her fears now 'wonderfully melted away'. Canada had frightened her too. 'I never had "spirit" for a wandering life...I know how very much of one's shrinking dread has all the unreality of fear of an unknown evil',[19] her mother learned just as they were coming home.

The difficulties of colonial life and an impractical husband left her undaunted. While Rex was occupied with the army and his music, Ewing built furniture '– rustic – you understand!',[20] dug and planted the garden – she loved gardening – made curtains, put up wallpaper, 'not a difficult art when the rooms are low',[21] and decorated her rooms with much contrivance and some originality. She was thrilled with a bed valence she made 'of an old white petticoat and trimmed with black braid!'[22] – evidence of the immensity of Victorian petticoats. She painted a sitting room dark blue with a Turkish proverb round the top in Arabic, in black and white letters: 'You have come in peace – depart in peace.' Outside, she tried archery and tobogganing. The latter, at first, was alarming. Her toboggan held four; three ladies sitting cross-legged, held in place by a man's outstretched legs. They whizzed off at sixty miles an hour, jumping several feet in the air over bumps. 'I don't think I shall ever take *much* to it but shall have another try.' She had wrenched her arm falling off.[23]

Life was gloriously fulfilling and romantic. They slept huddled in a small bed, from which they observed the night sky with a telescope. They skulked in the kitchen garden at night, pretending to be unmarried lovers 'and there is a terrible duenna next door who may hear us and betray us!!!'[24] They sketched together, canoed by moonlight 'I the bows and he the stern', learned Hebrew (both were stimulated by new alphabets); read French novels (Balzac was 'not altogether edifying', but worthwhile for his 'brilliance'), and petted their adored dogs. Every day, she felt, they grew happier. The vicarage daughter sought a moral. 'GOD (she always spelt God in capital letters) sometimes disciplines by happiness as well as by trouble, & we ought only to doubly try to be good!'[25]

Accommodating such a saintly character in the family cannot have been easy – witness the evening dress saga. Mrs Gatty wanted to send her daughter a new evening gown, a gift Ewing considered needlessly extravagant. Far better, she said, to pass on one from her sisters. So she asked for Dot's old pink silk – 'it has seen a good deal of service' – and started dreaming of ways to refurbish it with black spotted tulle, a '*puffed* sort of skirt' and a pink and black sash. Rex liked her in pink, she said. Poor Dot, who still liked it too, stalled. Ewing wrote back in a lather of further unselfishness: 'I would not *for worlds* have her send me the pink silk – I am only so glad she is using it. I only meant that being so much smaller – I might perhaps make some use of the best parts she had *done with*. But I really don't want anything...'

Ewing preferred to help her family before herself. She was undemanding in a way that was in itself demanding. Her generosity made Dot feel uncomfortably guilty of being 'unscrupulous about accepting her presents, on the score that she 'liked' to give them!'[26]

Throughout the Canadian sojourn, Ewing sent contributions to her mother for *Aunt Judy's Magazine*, including 'Reka Dom' and 'Kerguelen's Land', stories for *Mrs Overtheway's Remembrances* that appeared in the magazine in instalments between 1866 and 1868, and as a book in 1869. *Mrs Overtheway* is the tale of orphan Ida, who lives with her remote uncle and insensitive nurse. Her sailor father, she hears, drowned. Ida's pretence that the old lady opposite is her friend comes true, and Mrs Overtheway tells her stories of her long-ago childhood. Ida's rapture in the old lady's memories underlines their joint isolation. Mrs Overtheway has outlived all those she loved; Ida has no one to love. Finally, Ida's father miraculously returns, takes Ida away, leaving the child another of Mrs Overtheway's remembrances. Avery comments: 'Ewing excelled at conveying a sense of the passing of time...the warmth of family affection and the intensity of one's feelings then, but here, where she mingled them with the *lachrimae rerum*, she touched greatness.'[27] 'Reka Dom', Russian for 'River House', was the name of a house in Devon that Ewing had fallen in love with as a child, and she and Rex named their first home in Canada after it. In 'Reka Dom', the child Mrs Overtheway and her family settle in a new house, once owned by a Russian family. The children discover relics of other children's play in the garden, in particular a little boy, Ivan, who they think died. Later, the young girl Mrs Overtheway finds Ivan, now a young man. They marry and live happily ever after, until his death, which she describes to Ida. In this story Ewing, far from home, evokes her affection for its memory, for merry families playing in gardens, and marks her awareness of the strength of her love compared with the fragility and impermanence of the objects of it.

It was difficult, however, to find time for everything. Domesticity kept Ewing just as busy as her writing. Like her mother who had fitted writing around family and parish demands, Ewing put wifeliness first. She told Mr Bell: 'literature is a profession as well as an amusement to me,' but it was a part, not *the* part, of her life. The exigencies of a roving army life and ill health left literature lagging second, which may have affected the quantity of her output, but not her standard. She was a perfectionist. To be satisfied with anything less than her literary best was impossible. Several times she had to ask her mother to wait for her due instalments for *Aunt Judy*. 'Word-painting is such a pleasure, like playing a game of skill I take such minute pains, and cut and polish.'

After Canada, the Ewings were posted to Aldershot, where they remained for eight years. During this time, Mrs Gatty died in 1873, a deep sorrow to Ewing. The near-permanent feeling of being settled in one place resulted in her most prolific period. She wrote three children's novels – *A Flat Iron for a Farthing*, illustrated by Helen Allingham (1870–71), *Six to Sixteen* (1872) and *Jan of the Windmill* (1872–3) – as well as around sixty short stories and some songs. Encampment life inspired the gallant military message of her most famous book, *Jackanapes*. Like other officers' families, the Ewings lived in a wooden hut, which she arranged with practised flair. She stuck woodcuts of Academy pictures all over the dining room walls, found the effect 'charming', and created a garden. Ewing flung herself into the regiment, helping Rex put on theatricals and concerts. Men, women and children adored her and confided in her. Ethel Smyth, then a teenager of parents also stationed at Aldershot, later observed she had 'discreet, semi-intellectual and wholly blameless flirtations' with several officers at a time. Ewing's appeal lay in her sympathetic honesty. Ethel unburdened herself to Ewing, worried she 'gushed'. Ewing comforted her: 'the habit of gush, like a habit of pious talk, without being necessarily absolutely insincere *is* very objectionable, and both make me feel awkward. But I like a little divine fire in affairs of the heart and the soul.'[28]

Divine fire she liked best in restraint. Rex, ever affable, taught teen-aged Ethel musical harmony, to the dismay of her father, General Smyth, who disliked Rex as much as he admired Ewing. The general was convinced that an officer with a red nose was a drunken blot on the army. (Ethel diagnosed a poor digestion.) General Smyth checked his rage in reverence to Ewing until he discovered an intemperate letter from Rex to Ethel. Harmony ceased forthwith. Ewing understood Rex's affection, generously allowing its *'genuineness'*, but deplored his lack of care for Ethel's reputation. 'I consider that while you might defy Mrs Grundy without damage to yourself, she *couldn't* and your impunity should not take advantage of her enthusiasm. You know that when my presence in the house satisfied etiquette, it satisfied me, and I left you to yourselves.' Though Ewing considered the double standards of male and female behaviour unfair, they were as immovable as the mores of her time that she upheld with every fibre. Only her iron control of herself and of Rex could steer them through emotional rocks.

Rex was an eccentric. Though in her just-engaged rapture, Ewing had described him as 'very clever, a beautiful musician – good linguist – well read – a dab at meteorology, photography, awfully fond of dogs, a good rider and...a *mesmerist!*', his carelessness unbalanced their relationship. She was the firm hand, allowing Rex, twelve years older, the controlled freedom of eternal boyhood. He was not one self to her but several, as her many names for him show – Dyk, Alistir, Sandro, Sasha, My Bingalee, Boykin, Bonnie, Carissimo. She also demanded myriad responses from him. She could be 'your own little child', 'your lilla wife', and a haranguing scold. Her frequent address, 'My Own Dear Husband Boy', describes exactly her see-saw pedestal and parental attitude.

After 1877, the Ewings left Aldershot and began the years of short postings around Britain. Endless packing, unpacking and arranging followed. It was Ewing who enquired about the insurance, the drains, the unforeseen, such as *'How long* is it since the Diptheria was in [the house?]' All accounts left Rex bewildered, from coal to the newspapers, but Ewing was used to coping. 'Just mention up to what date you paid it *if you know*, and I'll settle that'(1879). Her packing was an art-form. 'Pictures and glass and china and books and music and silver and homeopathic medicines are all beautifully dovetailed with linen and carpets and clothes.' Still, she needed his approval. In emotional moments, she wrote to him in baby talk. 'Oh I am so pleased you *ike* our itta nest now...I was *so* low all yest because you didn't *ikle* it' (1879).

Money was a continual worry, both the paucity of their combined earnings and Rex's forgetfulness in providing for her. She borrowed from her sisters until awkwardness became unbearable. In 1879 when Rex was posted to Malta, Ewing packed up the household, including her current manuscript, sent everything off, ready to follow him. If the anguish of being without her work and the unsettled feeling of homelessness were not enough, Rex's inefficiency infuriated her.

> Darling, I hope you will send me £10 more, before you get the luggage. I have paid the freight and the insurance to Liverpool. You won't have quite £4 to pay at your end. I told Dot that you told me you could always repay what she lent me over this affair, and you know you have never repaid her anything and I absolutely *must* get some clothes.

The Malta episode prompted the lowest phase of her life. Unwell before she set off, she was longing to join him. In October, she got as far as France, travelling alone. For this challenge to feminine etiquette she cared not a jot. In France, though, she had a complete collapse. Nausea, headaches, giddiness, backache and 'internal discomfort of the prolapse style' prostrated her, so that when eventually she dressed she still could not bear to put on her stays. Diney (her sister Undine) came out to nurse her, and took her back to England. Ewing was shattered. 'Write a comforting letter to your poor wife – and oh tell me *you will not learn to love me less from our being so long apart.'* Her emotion burst through in an unguarded moment. Back in England she regained self-control. 'We are neither of us such fools as to be unable to bear our share of disappointment.' Ewing liked prudence. She had decided not to risk dying by continuing her journey – a shaky *wagon-lit* to Marseilles followed by seventeen days' sail – nor would she waste money resting in France. Rex should not waste money either; he should stay in Malta's mild climate – so good for his chest. When better, she would join him later. Her unselfish practicality checked all other impulses. Meanwhile she fretted about mould attacking their packing; Government stores, she feared, were notoriously damp.

Ewing never went to Malta, and she and Rex were to be parted for four years. Her health was too uncertain, though she tried to remain active and hopeful. She sought medical advice and told Rex all; she had no private prudish inhibitions, though her public face was ladylike and reticent. Her experiences show

29

how nineteenth-century doctors automatically linked uterine problems to female 'nerves'. One doctor was an 'utter fiasco'.

> He ridiculed all I put before him as the whim of a nervous and literary lady. The climax came with the leeches about which I had been very nervous. He forced an instrument into me which, apart, from the agony, I am certain would have been injurious at half the size. I went through with it, leeches and all and have had a week of great suffering. It left me feeling I'd been torn to pieces.

Another, Favell, who forbade the journey to Malta, gave her *'enormous* doses of bromide' though assured her the cause was not gynaecological, diagnosing nerve disease nonetheless. Unsympathetic friends had thought her a *malade imaginaire*. This infuriated Ewing. 'I am as certain as I am here that I have never in my life erred on the side of giving way. Goodness knows I've had hysterics in plenty the last few years, but I've had them as any man or woman might from pain, exhaustion or nervous worry.'

Hysteria was considered as demeaning as it was debilitating, edging the sufferer dangerously near the brink of insanity. Showalter calls Victorian female hysteria 'the desperate communication of the powerless'.[29] Emotion, hysteria, loss of control all spoke of an excess that nice women shrank from. In 1866 a doctor confirmed the accepted fact: 'with women it is but a step from downright hysteria to overt insanity'.[30] No wonder that Ewing, despite a matter-of-fact acceptance of her outbursts, in the same breath claimed 'I am neither constitutionally nor acquiredly hysterical'. Hers were an involuntary plea for Rex, her marriage, and an understanding of her suffering that good behaviour and the reticence of her nature forbade her to voice.

From Florence Nightingale who, post-Crimea, lay in bed while directing government policy on hospitals, to Coolidge's popular *What Katy Did* (1872), in which paralysed young Katy holds the moral and economic strings of the household in her frail hands, the nineteenth-century invalid woman could wield a position of strength from apparent weakness. Her very fragility rendered her character the more praiseworthy and persuasive. As another invalid, Christina Rosetti, said, 'I am very well content with the privileges and immunities which attach to semi-invalidism'.[31] Now established as an invalid, not a malingerer, invalidism itself an approved female state, at last Ewing felt comforted, and her hysterics ceased.

Ewing had been in England alone for nearly a year when Favell delivered the Malta blow in September 1880. She was devastated. She began a calm letter to Rex about her walks and a lovely sunset, until she suddenly couldn't hold on any more. 'Dykie! Dykie! I mayn't go!!'; a rare collapse of constraint. It was a bad time; other worries had meanwhile been mounting up. Rex's attractive personality brought him friends, and Ewing responded generously. 'You do strike me as having been very fortunate in the number of your 'affinities'.' She let him like women she liked too, but a lady in Malta failed to please her at all. Worse, Rex had been secretive. In March 1880 she delivered a broadside.

> My failing to appreciate ER was – simply – that I disbelieved in her. I did not want you to help ER to play the fool. I am still quite unconvinced that she *was worth* the sympathy you gave; and as we have always read and shown each other anything worthy of note in our friends' letters, it was perhaps not unnatural that I never thought there could be much beyond egotism in piles of letters of which you would never read me a line.

When Rex became ill in April, Ewing, with a headache from 'shock', instantly stopped scolding, pining to be his *'Faithful Nuss'*. 'My Pet! My Own! It is so hard to be patient *for oo.'* Rex needed a truss and Ewing, ever practical, was 'anxious that you should have a truss to *perfectly* suit you. I know over feminine affairs of the kind that if the "appliances" *fit* and *suit* the relief is said to be intense, and if they don't it makes matters worse.' Recovered, he wanted to go yachting, and Ewing encouraged him. 'The very thing for you, if it is possible to afford it.' But money remained a nagging problem. She appealed to Rex in baby-talk, her private language for deep feeling and her plea for reassurance.

> Had horrid visions that *you* were living 'on tick' in Malta – unpaid mess bills, like Aldershot. Worry – supposing he was ill/rainy day, or supposing her boy to die and leave her a mis lonely one, she would have to sell everything she had to pay off and then go into the workhouse – and if her boy were ill she could nit make him comfy for want of minlins and couldn't work to earn more. Now you must not be anglins with your wiff but let her tell you her troubles...It is

31

that you are so *unworldly*. I like you to say we will manage somehow *between us.*

During these débâcles, perhaps because of them, Ewing continued working. In October 1879 she began to serialize *Jackanapes*, her most famous work, for *Aunt Judy's Magazine*, published in book form in 1883. The tale hangs on the framework of the grey goose on the village green who watches Jackanapes, a bold, bright, brave yellow-haired boy, brought up spiritedly by his great aunt, Miss Jessamine. His friend is nice but dull Tony, one of many children of a fussy mother. Jackanapes is the orphan offspring of an elopement and grandson of a gallant general who buys him his heart's desire, Lollo, the gypsy's uncontrollable red pony. Jackanapes tames Lollo, who accompanies him years later to the war. Jackanapes is killed: when all around are retreating, he pulls wounded Tony, also a soldier, onto Lollo's back, saving his life at the cost of his own. The village cobbler provides the dissenting voice, seeing only foolhardiness and vainglory, pointing out that Tony's mother could more easily spare a child than Miss Jessamine. The story contrasts self-seeking with honourable traditions, while it is also a paean to rural England. Finally, gaffers and the aged grey goose on the green watch ancient Lollo pulling a very old Miss Jessamine in her bath chair, still cheerful and proud of her nephew's glorious death.

The book was wildly popular, initially selling 500 copies a day, though the quirks of Ewing's publishing arrangements gave her only a halfpenny on a shilling book. It struck a chord on publication as the Prince Imperial, shortly before, had been killed fighting in Africa, and the officer with him was much discussed for not saving him. 'A Grade' Jackanapes who sacrifices himself for 'C Grade' Tony symbolizes both a military code of glorious honour and a Christian message of sacrifice. Ewing rings the bell with the text for Jackanape's funeral sermon: 'Whosoever shall lose his life for My sake shall find it,' and her conclusion: 'There is a heritage of heroic example and noble obligation, not reckoned in the wealth of nations, but essential to a nation's life: the contempt of which may mean even its commercial fall.'

The story sprang from her depths. Though she felt she and Rex were equal partners, and was glad that he did not control her 'artistic career by the English church marriage service', nevertheless she herself breathed heroic sacrifice. Rex served his country, she, wifely, supported Rex, never complaining of ill-health, or little money, or the lack of settled life that helped her writing flow, only occasionally sighing '*How* nissy it would be to be *well!*'

She gave precise directions to her illustrator Randolph Caldecott, having, as a capable artist herself, an exact idea of how she wanted his lines to support her words; for instance: 'Give me one sketch of an almost baby lad learning to ride on a donkey (but not, oh *not!!!* at the seaside.)' 'Nothing', she concluded, 'is so hard as to extract the pathos that lies beneath 'Philistinism'. She sought within the jolliness of his drawings the sense of sadness that impregnates her light, robust style of writing – an echo, this, of the sense of privation permeating her own life that she refused to countenance. Caldecott, who became a firm friend, and his 'delicate dexterity' delighted her. Caldicott was bowled over by Ewing's charm, rejecting overtures by other authors. '"Lewis Carroll" did me the honour to apply to me the other day; but he did not flatter me as you do.'[32] They vied with each other in niceness. Ewing wanted Caldicott to charge enough to remunerate him well. Caldicott acknowledged he could easily charge more, 'supposing I wished to accumulate lucre…yet I should like to illustrate *Jackanapes* to your satisfaction…It will pay me somehow'.[33] He illustrated, as well as *Jackanapes*, *Daddy Darwin's Dovecot* and *Lob-Lie by-the Fire*, though, like Ewing, he suffered from ill-health and died the year after her.

Yonge advocated *Jackanapes* as a book for boys, but advised adults reading it aloud to skip the elopement – an 'unnecessary incident'.[34] For Ewing, moral but not prudish, herself the granddaughter of an elopement, it represented a healthily romantic enchantment that she insisted Caldecott make a picture of. 'We *must* have [it]. A very pretty elopement please! Finger post pointing to Scotland – Captain *not* in uniform of course.' She had, after all, married Rex in the teeth of family criticism. Love, sacrifice and heroism, the crux of *Jackanapes*, ruled Ewing utterly, but the ideals of her books differed from her own dealings. She let Jackanapes take risks, die and go to glory, but was too practical to risk her own life for love. 'Not to do what one wants is a hard lesson,' she told Rex, when she was forbidden to go to Malta. She forced herself to accept their separation patiently. Her circumspection was her heroic gesture and her homage to the altar of female submission.

After Malta, Rex was posted to Ceylon in 1881, even more impossible for Ewing. He remained there until 1883, while Ewing constantly searched for an improvement in cheap lodgings all over London. 'Dot has heard of some rooms kept by an old servant of Lady Harriet L–' in Finborough Road; in Sheffield Terrace 'drains were put in order last year'. Her independence meant lonely decisions; her health fluctuated, money was short. She stayed at Ecclesfield, and with friends, scrutinizing each sojourn; for instance: 'A Lady Bailey I met wants me to go and live with her at Ascot...Rooms for £2 a week and glorious air, but I did not take sufficiently to her to live under her wing...I like Sir Edward – a scientific and intelligent old bloke.' Drains and air were important issues for an invalid, susceptible to the miasmas that poor plumbing and position were known to carry. She begged Rex for enough to keep her '*in the same comfort in which you live yourself*', assuring him of her economies, 'mending my lilla chemise and under things to make them do a lilla longer', but as usual she put his interests first. 'Can you understand, my Dyk, how when I am 'not ki well' myself – every letter that tells me you are well is beyond words thank worthy?' She carried on writing to eke out income.

On visits home the Yorkshire countryside recalled her happy childhood. She recreated its landscape in *Daddy Darwin's Dovecote* (1881), a fulfilling tale of a country workhouse boy adopted by a grumpy pigeon-fancier who bequeaths him his house and land. Her hero could enjoy in perpetuity the beloved scenery and security of her childhood. She published some verse books in 1881, using poems she had written earlier. Constructed in Ogden Nash-like lines of unexpected lengths and rhyming patterns, they were amusing, popular and brought in some cash. *Laertes Sorte Mea, or The Story of a Short Life* appeared in 1882. In this sentimental, Victorian death-and-comfort tale, set in her familiar army territory, beautiful, active, suddenly crippled little Leonard dies a lingering, inspiring death. The title's translation, 'Happy is my lot', is Leonard's family motto that he strives to emulate in living and dying; an optimistic, insistent attitude close to Ewing's heart. Her description of Leonard's patience: 'That Leonard bore his sufferings better helped to conceal the fact that they undoubtedly increased,' has an autobiographical ring. She liked to be as profound and as tear-jerking as possible, and was delighted to hear that her story made two young barristers cry 'reading it aloud to each other in the Temple'.[35]

At last came news of Rex's return. Ewing, though still enduring violent headaches, enjoyed a surge of renewed energy. She rushed around, going to the Academy, getting her photograph taken, creating their new home, the Villa Ponente, near Taunton. Rex still kept forgetting her allowance, though she reminded him she was desperate and had never cost him much. Her shortages did not stop either her ready forgiveness or her shopping – 'I must let it out. I got two charming Dutch marquetry chairs for my drawing room for 35 shillings each...' In Devon she made a garden, digging it herself, and wrote *Mary's Meadow* (1883) about a family of gardening children, described by Laski as 'a most satisfying and enchanting story for gardeners of any age'.[36]

Early in 1885, painful 'neuralgia' brought her to bed, though she fully expected to recover, as a note to Rex attests: 'Your little child, *not* a poor one and quite well now,' though her wild, frail pencil scrawl suggests a different tale. Her last three months were an agony. Diagnosed with 'a species of blood poisoning', as her sister Dot called it, she went to Trull, near Bath for a change of air. There she died after two operations. Dot's account of Ewing's last weeks echoes the religious, lingering endings of one of her own tales. Ewing said her intolerable pain was sent from God for a purpose and she would use it to practise patience. Reading a fan letter a few days before she died, she said, 'I lead such a useless life, and there is so little I can do, it is a great pleasure to know I may have done *some* good.' The book she most enjoyed on her deathbed was Mark Twain's *Huckleberry Finn* because it made her laugh. Ewing's piety, modesty and quiet endurance was always punctuated by her sense of fun.

Ewing kept a commonplace book in which her final entry was strikingly apt. 'If we still love those we lose, can we altogether lose those we love?' Now forgotten except as a literary historicity, she is an almost extinguished echo of her age, though her books trail a legacy to the future in her view of children and childhood. Amongst the tears and the jingoism are winds of a modern air: ironic, individualistic, sensitive but not too serious, moral but not too religious. In the ideals Ewing hid in her fairy stories, and values she propounded in her family tales, she presents optimism, humour, practicality and, above all, wholesomeness.

She was buried at Trull. In 1886, the year after her death, Rex married one Elizabeth Margaret Cumby. Ewing knew widowers frequently remarried. Her father had married again aged 71, nine years after her mother's death – 'a bad business', Ewing thought. Always selfless about Rex's happiness, she would perhaps have been glad for him. In the fullness of time Rex and the second Mrs Ewing were buried in the same grave as the first. Ewing's last resting place made her niece, Undine's daughter, 'uneasy...I feel it is not what she would have chosen'.[37] During her mother's last illness, Ewing told Rex how she loved the Ecclesfield church where she had been christened, confirmed and, most joyful of all, married: 'O best of boys!...So very short a time and Boykin and wiffy will be "with those who rest" – I am almost weak enough to wish at Ecclesfield.' Nothing for Ewing ever turned out quite as she might have wished. Even so, nothing ever stopped her perceiving Jerusalem as golden.

WITH MILK AND HONEY BLEST

Mrs Gatty thought her daughter's work better and fresher than her own. In 1865, Ewing produced a horror story, *The Mystery of the Bloody Hand*, for the *London Magazine*. Her mother commented, 'I do not think she will write much more for children. It appears to me that the higher flight suits her best.' For reasons unknown, Ewing's 'higher flight' failed to materialize; her work was, apart from this one outburst, aimed at children.

She was highly esteemed by her contemporaries. Molesworth found in her writings 'the closeness of *herself*: her books are true exponents of her pure and faithful nature'.[38] Yonge thought them 'too delicately worked for the ordinary style of children of the poor', decidedly upper-class and 'exquisite'.[39] 'Real literature', said a contemporary critic, Edward Salmon.[40] Ewing herself derived from her work, as well as income, a story-telling fulfilment, an escape from cares, and a deep-felt need to promulgate the sources of her path to happiness. Likewise many of her stories show happy children making the best of unhappy circumstances. *A Flat Iron for a Farthing* (1870), the first and arguably best work of her domestic genre, is told by the motherless only-child hero, Regie. Nothing very unusual happens. Regie, a pleasant boy, has an affectionate father, dog, nurse, tutor, cousins, goes to school, and finally marries a girl whom coincidentally he had once seen buying a toy when both were children.

Beneath this rambling structure is an ironic analysis of nineteenth-century mores. Regie is heir to the squire of a rural English village, an apparently halcyon position shattered, as the book opens, with the death of his mother and stillborn sister. The village relies precariously on paternalism and the squire. Religious and determined to justify his privileged role, Regie nurses an infectious cottage boy and consequently nearly dies of fever. He gives his savings to a 'blind' con-man beggar, and learns he must temper generosity with realism. Being good, Ewing shows, can backfire. She pokes fun at petty piety. Regie and his cousin Polly, a bold, active girl who confounds the fragile-female image, climb a tree on Sunday – forbidden joy – justifying themselves by pretending the tree is a church, gabbling a 'sermon', and create merry havoc at the top ringing the dinner bell in the 'belfry'. Regie's mentor is the rector, brilliant and handsome. After his death Regie discovered his lower-class background.

Every circumstance in the book has layers of implication as Ewing jolts icons of expectations, a reflection of Victorian thinking that fluctuated in doubt. Acts of Parliament: Education Acts, Poor Laws, Reform Bills had brought political change; Darwin's *Origin of Species* was revolutionary and religion-challenging; the European revolutions of 1848 invited new thoughts about old political economy; new science and new criticism undermined old convictions; the industrial revolution created a new sense of speed and a nouveaux riches class. As the philosopher Mill said in 1854, 'It requires in these times much more intellect to marshal so much greater a stock of ideas and observations. Those who should be guides see too many sides to every question...They feel no assurance of the truth of anything.'[41] *A Flat Iron* mirrors a sea of moral and social uncertainties and offers a lifeline of cheerful endeavour.

In forefronting the character of Regie's Nurse Bundle, Ewing explores the import of the nurse on Victorian childhood. By 1850, a nurse had become an essential marker of class to aspiring families. In one sense children and servants, relegated to back parts of the house, given plain, economical food, both better seen but not heard, were bracketed in inferiority. The conundrum in which the child, offspring of the ruling class, was superior to the working-class woman in charge of him/her, was a situation that called for silent understandings of the rules of class learned early. *The Spectator* put it succinctly: 'The servant looks up to her little charges because they are of a rank above her own.'[42] The best type of nurse was thought to be, like Nurse Bundle, one who combined a perceived working-class simple rurality with a middle-class behavioural outlook.

The nurse fulfilled much of Ruskin's vision of female perfection; she was 'guardian of the hearth', dependant, devoted, enhancing a pure image of childhood. In practice, the nurse actually displaced the mother in day-to-day care, while the mother wore the crown of domestic queen, another example of the Victorian ability to say one thing under the cover of another. The nurse/child relationship was complicated as it bent to accommodate the class system. Though based on the closest possible intimacy, there was a yawning class chasm ever present that opened fully at the close of childhood when the child left the nursery. Molesworth's child novels show the frustrations of the nurse whose lowly position prevents her speaking out publicly to help the child, making the link between child and nurse strong but secretive, but Molesworth, unlike the wholesome Ewing, enjoyed investigating intricate emotionalism. Stevenson underlined the impact of his own nurse on him in his dedication to her in *A Child's Garden of Verses* (1885): 'My second Mother, my first Wife/ The angel of my infant life.'

Nurse Bundle's place in children's literature is unique. Inspired by Ewing's father's nurse, she is the first good nurse to dominate a children's book. Wise, loving, she epitomizes security and morality. Known by her job-description and surname, however, she lacks any other identity. A surname-only woman was, to the Victorians, inferior. 'Good old Bundle,' enthused *The Spectator*'s 1896 review of *A Flat Iron*, at once raising and diminishing her. Nevertheless, Regie's childhood reliance and adult regard establishes the lifelong debt owed by the child to the servant, a see-saw of class enigmas that Ewing reflects in her domestic tales.

Ewing's sound, matter-of-fact approach helped one unhappy child. Kipling, sent from a halcyon Indian babyhood to unhappy exile in England, loved her works. He read *Six to Sixteen* aged 7 when it first appeared in 1872. 'I owe more to that tale than I can tell. I knew it, as I know it still, almost by heart. Here was a history of real people and real things.'[43]

Though Ewing introduced it as 'a sketch of domestic life, not a vehicle for theories', the book discusses female upbringing. *Six to Sixteen* is the story of Margery Vandeleur, orphaned in circumstances that Burnett later borrowed for *The Secret Garden* and *A Little Princess*. Margery's pretty mother, more devoted to parties than parenthood, dies in an Indian cholera epidemic, thus disposing of one kind of mothering. The entire regiment also succumbs, an episode Ewing based on Rex's early army experiences in China but switched to a more topical empire setting. Margery leaves her Indian servants, is upset by a pithy Mrs Minchin, passed from pillar to post, ending up happily in the Yorkshire moors. Margery is sent to her conventional aunt, whose own daughter Matilda suffers from her unimaginative methods, growing moody and unsociable, thus condemning another kind of mothering. The children are educated disastrously by a governess and at school until finally Margery finds a happy home with her friend Eleanor.

Ewing's attack on girls' education can be read as a plea for female re-evaluation. The early nineteenth century classed women, children and lunatics under the same legal umbrella of incompetence. The Married Women's Property Act, allowing women control over their money, was not enforced until 1882. The prevailing view that since female brainpower was inferior to male, women needed less education, kept women back. Yonge's hymn to female scholarly surrender in *The Daisy Chain*, when Ethel May renounces classics, is well known. Middle-class girls were, for the most part, educated by a governess, who was a metaphor for Victorian female vulnerability. Female status and the governess fed each other inferiority. Governessing was one of the few acceptable means to a living for ladies, though, badly paid and uneasily not part of the family, they were, as Charlotte Brontë experienced, marginalized. The usual curriculum was limited – 'English grammar, history, use of the globes, French, perhaps Italian, piano, singing, drawing'[44] – mere accomplishment, directing girls to the marriage market rather than to marketable skills, and perpetuating the dependent female image. Governess novels abounded in Victorian Britain, while in real life, as Horn points out, the governess 'gripped the imagination [which] tells us much about the aspirations and anxieties of the Victorians'.[45]

The governess in *Six to Sixteen* 'filled our poor little empty heads with a great deal of folly' and was quickly dismissed. The school chosen instead is worse than the governess. Bush House is the sort of small, select, 'finishing' establishment that became popular in the second half of the nineteenth century, described by a contemporary educationalist as 'not so much an educational agent as a tribute which the parent pays to his own social position'.[46] Ewing deplored select schools with poor standards. Molesworth, her contemporary, liked serious, academic girls but was wary of all schools since they aimed instruction at career-aspiration, thus, she felt, curtailing a good, broad education, while also mixing classes overmuch. An acceptable balance was hard to find in a world that craved rules, and in which old standards were clung to as fast as they changed into new. At Bush House the healthcare is as bad as the teaching. Poor Matilda becomes consumptive and is removed, while Margery finds happiness with her friend Eleanor's family who pursue fresh air and self-education in 'intellectual hobbies' such as seaweed research and writing – Ewing's affectionate recall of her own childhood. *Six to Sixteen* ends by comparing intellectual fulfilment with religious consolation, a measure of Ewing's passion. In her domestic tales she never demanded a revolution in female education, but she pushed hard against current convention which she saw as foolish, frivolous, and ultimately demeaning to women.

In her fairy tales, unconstrained by realist fetters, Ewing created her utopian vision. Here at last are strong-minded, clever females. The Victorian fairy tale flowered as writers converted its ancient literary function of social commentary into a criticism of current mores and vehicle of visionary ideals. As Zipes has noted, writers such as Carroll, Macdonald, Ewing and Molesworth 'used the fairy tale as a radical mirror to reflect what was wrong',[47] subverting the classical stronghold of Perrault, the Grimms and Andersen by injecting their concerns into traditional tales of transformation and aspiration. 'They expanded the fairy-tale discourse on civilization to conceive alternate worlds and styles of life.'[48] They questioned authority, the structure of society, the restrictions of upbringing and notions of masculinity and femininity. They showed both in need of compassion, strength of character, and self-determination.

'My *aim*', Ewing said, 'is to imitate the "old originals"'.[49] The ideas behind the old tales were, she felt, universal, 'such as the idea of the weak outwitting the strong', to which she added her own reformist concerns. All real fairy tales, she thought, 'shld [*sic*] be written as if they were oral traditions taken down from the lips of a "story-teller"', which made her 'cut out reflections, abandon epithets, & shorten sentences';[50] thus *Amelia and the Dwarfs* purports to come from 'my grandmother's grandmother'. *The Land of Lost Toys* pretends to be told by reliable Aunt Penelope, and all are written in a snappy style. 'I do not believe that wonder-tales confuse the child's idea of truth',[51] said Ewing, planting her ideals through her magic setting. In *The Ogre Courting* (1871) Managing Molly, a peasant's clever daughter, outwits a rich ogre so that she gets his money and he never gets her. The giant likes small women who are good housewives, though all his many previous wives died mysteriously. Alarm bells ring at the vulnerability of Little Women homemakers. Molly reverses the image. She pretends to be so house proud that the ogre, having eagerly handed over his worldly goods, is put off and bolts during the engagement. Now well-dowered Molly can marry as she pleases. Ewing throws the female icon back in a male face, while showing empowerment can lie within an intelligent and manipulative female grasp.

In *Amelia and the Dwarfs* (1870) horrid, spoiled little Amelia is stolen by dwarfs and punished for ill-temper by hard labour underground. Reformed, she escapes back home. Amelia illustrates another kind of poor mothering: indulgency. 'My dear-r-r-Ramelia!' is her mother's severest reprimand. Ewing mockingly uncovers the contrivances of gracious living so affectionately drawn by Gaskell in *Cranford*, in which ladies in reduced circumstances keep up appearances. Amelia's snoops at her neighbours reveal shameful household secrets: glued china, a humble box disguised as an ottoman. Amelia learns to cope with this world of manners in which image is all and honesty is impolite by going underground. In the dwarfs' caverns she is reformed by hard work, a holy Victorian trinity of zeal, dedication and purification. Carlyle saw all workers as magnificently masculine, 'one grand Host...noble every soldier in it'.[52] Female labourers belied the concept of Victorian femininity; in 1862 the reforming Shaftsbury's investigative reports into labouring women found them bold and masculine-looking. But Amelia escapes definitions, crossing class and sexual boundaries, using trickery with her feminine charms, exploiting the dwarfs' male carnality. In their subterranean lair she learns to field a sinister dwarf's overtures with subterfuge, and uses trickery to escape. Back home, everyone finds her gentle, a conformist mask that covers her capabilities. She is 'unusually clever as those who have been with the Little People are said always to be'. The fairy tale setting, unlike a realist one, sanctions a clever, manipulative and strong-minded heroine who steers through a rapacious male world and polite society.

Ewing, anti-authority, sides with the child. *The Land of Lost Toys* (1869) is a nightmare story of adult Aunt Penelope, suddenly in the power of her childhood doll, Rosa, who says with a sinister smile that she will treat her ex-owner just as she had been used herself. Aunt Penelope mistakenly thinks she is safe. In pay-back Rosa forces Aunt Penelope to behave irrationally. She is cruel and insensitive while professing love. Ewing shows the child to be a plaything of adult whim, its individuality and integrity overlooked by well-meaning, obdurate adults in the name of upbringing. Ewing's stories are full of good children with parents in the wrong. Fathers are irascible, mothers make mistakes. Ewing's good child, a left-over of eighteenth-century Rousseau Romanticism, questions parental authority, the microcosm of Victorian paternalism, reflecting the doubt that riddled Victorian thinking.

For Ewing, the answer to doubt was optimism. She met the difficulties of her marriage with patience. Whether she faced her unhappiness and decided to overcome it, or whether she deliberately ignored it, her response was a mask of buoyancy that hid feeling behind stoicism. Both mask and optimism required self-sacrifice, the by-product of the religious and army traditions of her upbringing and marriage, as well as a womanly yielding to male superiority. All formed a monument to the expectations of her age. As Christina Rossetti put it:

> Lord, give me grace
> To take the lowest place.[53]

Ewing inserted a very different female image into her fairy tales. Only magic could reveal a better world beyond the mask of convention.

3

Mary Louisa Molesworth

The sunshine is there, though it is sometimes so veiled
to us

('Story-Writing', *Monthly Packet*, 1894)

She was the most popular children's writer of her day. Her
output was phenomenal. Between 1870 and 1911 Molesworth
produced over a hundred books, family and fantasy stories for
children from the nursery to young adulthood. Her literary
vision of late nineteenth- and early twentieth-century childhood
is uniquely realist, and representative of middle-class attitudes.
The Times obituary eulogized, 'During not far short of half a
century [she] has given happy thoughts to childhood. Mrs
Molesworth's books have not been superseded, and very likely
never will be.'[1] Salmon, a contemporary critic, called her 'the
best story-teller for children England has yet known'.[2] 'No-one
ever did understand children like you,' said her friend, the poet
Swinburne.[3] To understand the convolutions of any age, there
can be no better introduction than the morals and mores
inculcated into its young. There is no better insight into the
manoeuvres of the Victorian mind than Molesworth's child
novels. Here are the clashing modes of thought that underpinned the Victorian battle between convention and individuality, between self-development and self-sacrifice.

Molesworth presents a two-pronged 'is' and 'ought' approach
to childhood. Her characters strive for an ideal, a middle-class
haven-home made of mammas, papas, children and good
behaviour. Beneath this golden veneer she reveals a gaping
crack: the conflict between homage to the family and self-
fulfilment. To promote the happy family she analyses unhappy

families. Her anarchic children are unhappy because they are unloved; her cure lies in parents and children controlling themselves. Molesworth understood but did not allow temper and frustration. Her own life contained tragedy, but she made her own luck, capitalizing on her determination and talent. In her books her hope of familial bliss is steeped in autobiographical sincerity, in which disillusion is recognized but hidden, while endeavour reigns triumphant. It encapsulates the nineteenth-century middle-class view of itself, and accounts for her half-century of now vanished popularity.

A CLOSED BOOK

Molesworth's life was composed of secrets. True to Victorian form, which swept irregularities under the carpet, hers were well concealed. She appeared the very acme of respectability. The daughter of Scottish parents – Agnes, née Wilson, and Charles Stewart – she was born in Rotterdam, where her father was a merchant. Her mother belonged to a big, happy, wealthy, landowning family from Fifeshire. Her father was the illegitimate son of a girl intended for domestic service, Isabel Innis, who instead caught the roving eye of an army officer, William Stewart. William had several other illegitimate children by servant girls. All bore his name and had his financial help. Later he became extremely reputable as Lieutenant-Governor of New South Wales and a major general, with a wife and legitimate family. Charles Stewart lived with his mother, who subsequently married, family legend told, a 'vicious' man. Isabel left him, a pattern that was to be repeated by her granddaughter, and returned to domestic service as a housekeeper in Rotterdam. Isabel's employer gave Charles a job in his firm, paving the way from the boy's *mésalliance* background to his rise to respectable middle-class prosperity.

Illegitimacy was an appalling slur on Victorian reputation. Charles told his wife but not his children. He was bitterly hurt when his father told him he must never look on his legitimate half-sisters as his blood relations. As a child, Louisa, known as Louie, knew nothing of this, and was informed only in adulthood that a mystery hung about her father's origins. She told her children that her father was possibly the illegitimate son of the Duke of Sussex, based on the flimsy evidence that both bore the name Augustus. 'I think it wrong of me to want to know the whole story,' she told a close friend in middle age.[4] Curiosity killed the cat, Victorians were led to believe. Too much Stewart family knowledge might have killed all pretensions to gentility. The servant grandmother and the humdrum, not royal, illegitimacy posed a secret that held Louie fast to middle-class respectability.

Her parents left Holland when she was two. Not well off, with a family of six children (Louisa was the third), they lived in a small house in smoky, industrial Manchester. In her books Molesworth often made a dingy exterior contrast with warmth within. 'What matters most to children is not where their home is, but what it is.'[5] The Stewarts' was a stronghold. Once, aged six, during a drive on a stormy night with her parents, the carriage stopped. The coachman had run off. The terrified child was comforted by her mother. ' "Don't you see Papa is driving?" I shall never forget the impression of absolute comfort and fearlessness that came over me. "Papa is driving. We are quite, quite safe." '[6]

Molesworth felt her strength sprang from her childhood. She wanted her books to radiate a similar mantra of parental love – 'God-given, a shelter and support' – to sustain her child readers in adolescent disillusionment – 'the gradual discovery that neither father nor mother is infallible', when they should feel 'sympathy', based on the 'bonds of old childish love'.[7] By the time she wrote this her own children were survivors of parental fallibility. During their teens Molesworth had left their father, removed them to France, pretended to be a widow, worked furiously to earn her living by writing, giving them an irregular marital background couched in untruthfulness. Though such irregularity might have jeopardized social status, Molesworth pursued single-mindedly the position she felt due to herself and her children. Back in London, her sons were launched in professions, her daughters were presented in drawing rooms at Buckingham Palace, her friends were intellectual, literary and fashionable. Her children admired and loved her, their 'sympathy' unquestioned. Her mixture of understanding, charm, determination, hard work and absolute belief in the rightness of her stance saw her through potentially insuperable obstacles.

Molesworth encapsulates the ethos of Samuel Smiles's *Self-Help, with Illustrations of Conduct and Perseverance* (1859). This mid-century runaway best-seller extolling individuals' self-propelled rise from obscurity to riches was in many homes almost as revered as the Bible. Smiles argued that 'self-respect, application, industry, integrity' – his formula for success – were habits that must be acquired.[8] Molesworth's domestic children's books concur. 'It is only your own self, earnestly wishing to be good, that can really make you succeed.'[9] 'Bad habits are seldom to be uprooted at once; they are terribly clinging! But so are good ones – a week of steady perseverance in doing a right thing, small though it may be, is something like "compound interest".'[10] 'Being good grows.'[11] In her fairy stories, her heroines succeed through tenacity. 'A Fairy House'[12] illustrates her belief in detail and diligence. A fairy had to build a house with a heap of stones. When it was nearly finished she saw it leant slightly to one side, but hoped the fairy queen, inspecting it, wouldn't notice. The sharp-eyed queen made her begin again. The fairy found and added a tiny, missing stone which made the shining edifice perfect. Now the queen gave it to her as a reward.

Molesworth and Smiles lived through years of massive, silent, social change. They saw the demise of the aristocracy and the efforts of the industrial middle classes to achieve the money, land and titles of the former. The volatile economic climate of the last quarter of the nineteenth century meant that middle-class stability was itself unreliable. Families prospered and collapsed. Molesworth's child texts reflect a world of desirable but precarious security, in which new opportunities and old standards of class coexist uncomfortably. Riddled with moral homilies, they inform with an earnestness close to anxiety. Frequently in her children's books she hints beyond the child's happy dénouement to adult disappointment. Her own life showed her that a happy childhood was no precursor of happy adulthood, and that hard work was a guarantee of success that could take a nobody to renown. She was as concerned to teach her child readers to persevere as she was to earn her living by so doing.

Molesworth was a serious, precocious child. Aged 6, she enjoyed Scott, despite his complicated prose. She also read but disliked Maria Edgeworth's books. 'I missed something – a lack of sentiment.'[13] She loved Wetherell's *The Wide, Wide World* (1852), an orphan tale drenched in emotion that she still found impossible to read in adulthood without tears. There was a part of Molesworth's nature that identified with angst. She remembered her childhood not for its events but for the 'inner childish life and intensities of feeling'[14] that inspired her texts. Feelings, not plots, were her strong point. Secretly she acted out emotional plays, in which her cast was composed of the cotton reels in her mother's workbox.

Her narrative zest came from her mother's family. Her maternal grandmother, who had beautiful white hands with strange shell markings, was a mesmerizing story-teller, and impressed her as frightening and fairy-like. The magical, wise, ruthless, old-while-eternally-young, story-telling grandmother figure is a recurring image in Molesworth's fantasy tales. Often a peasant, she links themes of time, faery and female power. She may have also had another source. Molesworth's childhood nurse was old Hannah Jenkinson, once employed by Dorothy Wordsworth, who returned to care for the elderly Wordsworths, miserable at leaving her small Stewart charges. Wordsworth wrote to 'little Louisa' on Hannah's behalf (she could not write), and sent her a present of a Stewart tartan neckerchief. Molesworth repeated the story of Hannah and William Wordsworth as a veneration of literature and agedness, like a legend to her own children.

As Louisa's ambitious father grew steadily richer, the Stewarts moved to bigger houses. In Manchester the Gaskells were neighbours when Louisa was in her early teens. William, the nonconformist clergyman and reforming educationalist, gave her lessons, making her translate to exercise precision of meaning, while his novelist wife encouraged her writing. She completed her education in France for two years, an unusually long absence for a young girl, the reason for which is lost. On her return, grown up, graceful and charming, she met Richard Molesworth.

Richard was a cavalry officer in the Royal Dragoons. Noted in military records for his heroic leadership in the Indian Mutiny and the Crimean War, his insouciance inspired his men's morale. Once in the heat of battle on a heavily defended

Crimean peak, he lit his cigar as shells exploded around him, till a shell splinter knocked it from his mouth. He was, Molesworth's sister reminisced, 'young, gallant, handsome – what girl could have resisted him?'[15] He was also aristocratic, a nephew of the seventh Viscount Molesworth. They married in 1861, both deeply in love, Louisa aged 22 and Richard 25, to the approval of all except Louisa's mother. Molesworth's social status now soared above her father's whiff of trade, while Richard's income, a captain's meagre pittance, was upped by his rich, generous father-in-law. However, his mother-in-law mistrusted his temper. He was subject to outbursts of rage. A post-mortem revealed shrapnel in his head, which may have accounted for them. But Molesworth, in full flush of love, youth and obstinacy, was convinced she could quell the storms. She was Richard's darling Louie, as his inscription in an engagement present book confirmed.

At first the Molesworths, like the Ewings, moved around army postings. Children arrived promptly, Violet nine months after the wedding and Cicely eight months later. In 1864 they rented Tabley Grange, near Knutsford in Cheshire, a large house on the estate of a much grander house belonging to an old Molesworth family friend, Lord de Tabley. By this time Molesworth knew she had made an irreversible mistake. She knew she was not always easy, that she could be fussy and fidgety, but she found Richard snobbish, unsociable and idle, his temper terrifying and unpredictable. She did her best to smooth over their jarring temperaments. By 1867, six years after marriage, she had four daughters, and three sons followed between 1869 and 1873.

Lord de Tabley had a bachelor son, John Warren, later the third Baron de Tabley, a poet and botanist. A few years older than Molesworth, he became her private emotional prop. Theirs was a peculiarly Victorian relationship, conducted along now-forgotten lines of correspondence, fervour and reserve. Their friendship had all the ingredients of a full-blown affair: concealment (they tried to stop the postman getting suspicious), jealousy (on Molesworth's part), confidences, private names (she called him Mr Redrose), fury over misunderstandings, and covert meetings. If they had sexual feelings for each other, however, they were well concealed. Molesworth appreciated her

49

obligations to position and feminine protocol; she thought it indelicate, even, to mention her impending childbirth to Warren. She continually reminded him: 'Pray remember always abt burning', instructions he invariably ignored.

Though there were some secrets 'I can never tell you',[16] she revealed others. The flaws in her marriage were profoundly depressing. She told Warren:

> My autobiography came to an end several years ago. It died and I buried it & it was the best thing to do. I became practical and middle-aged very young. My deepest experience of life is not of a kind that would ever make a romance. Pray do not think me very silly and affected. I am truly very middle-aged. [She was twenty-nine.] I am so ashamed of all this about myself.[17]

Her confidences never made her feel she betrayed Richard. 'Truly I am not [disloyal], though I may seem it.'[18] Nevertheless, she was determined to keep her friendship secret, telling Richard little fibs to protect them all, while she expiated on his shortcomings and demanded Warren's help. A typical comment:

> A great part of my unhappiness has been caused by disagreeables between my father and R in which I must say the latter has been the chief aggressor. I want you to be so truly kind to me as to try to soften his ideas as to class prejudice, dislike to society, sneering at anyone not exactly to his way of thinking. I could never tell you half what we owe to my father. Please be as good as you can.[19]

Molesworth's sister noted that Richard and Louie were much better tempered when Warren came to dine. Unfortunately he was easily upset. His friend Edmund Gosse declared, no one 'however tactful got through many years of Lord de Tabley's intimacy without an electric storm'.[20] It was Molesworth's bad luck that having found a kindred-spirit, she not only had to hide her closeness from the outside world, but watch every word, just as she did with Richard, though she refused to pander to Warren when she unwittingly upset him.

> You have taken immense pains to convince me, not ready to be convinced – that I had a place of my own…I claim its dues. I am not going to seem amiable and considerate and all that.[21]

The 'duck episode', as she called it, illuminates the quagmires she negotiated. Charles Stewart sent the de Tableys a brace of rare American wild duck, and Warren wrongly suspected toadying. Molesworth, furious with Warren, apologized haughtily on her father's behalf, though 'the thing should require no apology – rather the reverse'.[22] She knew if her father, a proud man, heard of Warren's reaction, he would forbid her to see the de Tableys, and Molesworth was as determined to save her friendship as to protect her father's honour.

Twentieth-century critics have found Molesworth's books rife with snobbery. In this they reflect her time. Verdicts about class dominated Victorian thought and behaviour. Molesworth herself loathed arrogance and prejudice. Sensitive to the nuances of a landed-gentry world, she was made to feel aware that her adored trade-background father had bought his way upwards. She resented the contempt with which the upper classes regarded the nouveaux riches, and admired the Darwinian struggle from the ranks to gentrification.

She loved, however, being part of the unassailable aura that she felt radiated from upper-class superiority. She makes a crude point in an adult short story, *The Sealskin Purse*.[23] Mrs Mallory is a social climber, whose lack of breeding is betrayed by 'the very faintest suspicion of a tone rather than accent' and 'loud, rather boisterous gaiety'. She wrongly accuses gentle, sweet Cecil Wode, the only daughter of Lord Mavor, of stealing her purse. Unmasking a bounder was a sport much enjoyed by Victorian upper-class players. Lilliputian and deadly were the weapons employed. Voice and bearing fatally revealed background only to the initiated. Upstart Mrs Mallory doesn't realize Cecil is a lady, dubs her a governess, a mere Miss Wood, ignorant of upper-class insider knowledge that Wood is Wode, the Mavor family name. When, at a ball, Mrs Mallory realizes who Cecil is, she faints with shock. Her fall from grace lands her flat on the floor. 'Don't prop her up,' says Cecil, dabbing her brow.

Molesworth's concern for correct behaviour went deeper than this burlesque. She linked class with morality, treating rules of behaviour with the awe of a religious acolyte. In this she was not unique. Nineteenth-century manners acted as a social directive. They upheld culture and tradition. Society was mercilessly unforgiving towards those who broke its taboos. Behaviour that contravened customs of either etiquette or sex could cast a perpetrator into a dead-end Bohemian pit of disrepute, while a ladylike girl was set fair for marriage, her respectability and her future assured.

Molesworth's child heroines' duty of self-improvement coincides with the moral duty they owe to their class. Molesworth dissects their attitudes under a microscope. In *Blanche* (1893), well-born Stacy refuses to accompany lower-class Florry for a walk. Blanche, Stacy's sister, deplores this 'worldly narrow-mindedness'.[24] Molesworth explains in *Silverthorns* (1887): 'It is the most ill-bred and vulgar idea to suppose that the right way of keeping people in their places is by being rude to them. That at once puts one beneath them.'[25] In *The Rectory Children* (1889), upper-class Biddy, the rector's daughter, is rude and lazy. Celestina, the shopkeeper's daughter, helps her reform. Celestina, self-controlled, gentle, quiet, has the ladylike qualities Biddy lacks, though she is warned by her father not to 'be getting any nonsense in your head of setting up to be the same as ladies' children'.[26] Molesworth's lower-class characters are often better behaved than her upper-class. Nevertheless she clung to the magical glow of 'something indescribable'[27] that she felt devolved on the upper classes. The attention paid to class in her texts reflects both the outlook of her age and appreciation of her own potentially precarious position. Her marriage constantly reminded her of upper-class distaste for her Manchester trade background, while her separation broke a convention that might have plunged a less determined woman into social ruin.

Molesworth had begun a novel, but burned it three times. Warren boosted her literary confidence, stopped Richard's disapproval of 'scribbling', and helped her final version, *Lover and Husband*, the story of an unhappy marriage, to the publishers in 1869, just after her eldest daughter died aged 6. This was Molesworth's most unhappy year. Violet died of scarlet fever while staying with Molesworth's parents. Her final hours were over so swiftly that her mother was unable to get to her. 'Agony beyond expression,' she told Warren. Her other three daughters were also ill, Cicely desperately so. She, ill herself, was heavily pregnant with her fifth child and first son, who died aged three months. Richard, frequently absent on army manoeuvres, she found unsupportive. She longed for death, though knew the wish was 'wicked'.

Tabley Grange now symbolized despair and she insisted on leaving it. They had spent a sizeable sum on improvements, which, since it was only rented, they lost. Molesworth did not care. She was equally determined to see her book published for Violet's sake. As precocious a 6-year-old as her mother had been, Violet had read some of it, and chosen some chapter titles. Warren had once noted her children did not interest her overmuch. Molesworth now realized how intensely she loved Violet; all her life she hallowed her memory. Soon after she died, Molesworth wrote a short story, 'Good-night Winny', for her first children's book, *Tell Me a Story* (1875). The tale of Violet's character and death from Cicely's point of view, it signals the way Molesworth identified with children and her recognition of child-feeling. Macmillan, her publishers, produced Walter Crane as illustrator. To Molesworth's delight he drew the highlights of her text, even remembering Winny's slippers left forlornly by her bed. It was the start of a series of sympathetic Crane illustrations, as well as a strong friendship. In 1890 Molesworth wrote a book featuring a Macdonald/North Wind-like figure, old/young, beautiful, stern, wise and magical. The book was to be entitled 'The Princess with the Forget-Me-Not Eyes', and chapter 1, describing the child heroines, to be called 'The Children of the Castle'. Crane got muddled, and illustrated the book's red cover with a castle's portcullis, incorporating the words 'The Children of The Castle' below the ramparts. Crane had no time to change his design, and Molesworth's good manners forgave all; his title and their friendship survived.

She defined her credo in writing about children, for children.

> It is more than the love of children. It is clothing your own personality with theirs, seeing as they see, realizing the intensity of their hopes and fears, yet remaining yourself, never losing sight of what is good for them.[28]

She scrutinized her child characters while she sought to improve them, a literary example of the Victorian frame of mind that inclined to moral earnestness and classification, which she stretched to affirm each child's uniqueness.

The success of *Tell Me a Story* (1875) prompted a family friend, Sir Noel Paton to opine: 'better do a small thing well than a greater thing indifferently'.[29] Her first four adult novels, all deconstructions of unhappy relationships, had received little critical attention. She followed his advice. *Carrots, Just a Little Boy* (1876) stormed the children's market, followed by the equally popular *The Cuckoo Clock* (1877). She was now hailed as a leading children's writer, on a par with Lewis Carroll, George Macdonald, and Charlotte Yonge. Though she continued to write for adults, her children's books easily outstripped their sales.

Molesworth thought *Carrots's* success sprang from its originality. Nothing like it had yet appeared for children. Six-year-old Fabian, nicknamed Carrots because of his red hair, is lambasted by his father for stealing a half-sovereign. When questioned, Carrots admits hiding a magical 'fairy yellow sixpence'. His father is going to beat him. Carrots is miserable and confused. He thinks a sovereign is a monarch, a half-sovereign muddles him completely. Carrots learns 'that saddest of all sad things – the way in which it is possible for our very nearest and dearest to misunderstand us',[30] and to be wary of his family. Here is no haven of happy middle-class security. The afterthought in a large, impoverished family, his birth makes everyone feel they could have done without him. His father is bad-tempered, very like, Cicely later said, her own father. His mother finds her six children hard to manage. Both are criticized. Molesworth had no compunction in undermining traditional patriarchal authority or debunking Ruskin's image of mother-goddess of the hearth. Instead she makes clear to adults and children in one breath, in her hallmark style of direct and urgent emotional appeal, the Rousseau-like innocence of childhood and the onerous responsibilities of parenthood.

> The 'own self' of Carrots...the 'soul', children, which is in you all...may grow into so lovely and perfect a thing may, alas! be twisted and stunted and starved out of all likeness to the 'image' in which it was created. Do you understand why it seems sometimes such a very, very solemn thing to have the charge of children?[31]

Her sympathy with her child characters advances their right to be understood; her proposition that parents fail, and her creed that the child nevertheless must see them as a 'God-given' support, confusingly supports and undermines the family structure.

The Molesworths were showing themselves as less than perfect parents themselves. It is impossible not to connect Molesworth's sensitivity to the link between child unhappiness and parental behaviour with her own family experience. The Molesworths now underwent a series of rapid house changes. The happy family home seemed impossible to find. They left Tabley for another Cheshire house in 1870, went to Wales in 1875, four months later settled in Edinburgh and finally moved to France in 1877. Richard returned to Britain; Molesworth did not. She kept the children, and began a seven-year sojourn abroad, passing herself off as a widow. Her mother, a genuine widow, joined her. The separation was approved by Richard's family, and Molesworth remained on amicable terms with them.

Even abroad she was restless, moving from Pau to Caen to Paris to Coburg, and back again to Paris. Molesworth always said she had no particular attachment to place, and preferred continental heat to gloomy British weather. The decision to live in France, made easier by her fluency in French, presumably eased her path with anonymity.

Her life changed course. Remarriage was unthinkable; respectability demanded a celibate life. Hers now revolved around children and writing. Her friendship with Warren faded. When he went travelling in 1870, Molesworth reminded him:

> You do know if you the least feel inclined to pull your end of the wire, I shall always be ready at the other. I hope you will remember it – Even if you don't, it will make no difference in the fact.[32]

But, her overtures ignored, they lost touch. Two years after her return to London, still nurturing fond memories, she asked him to call. 'Up to four o'clock the chances are you will find me alone.' Warren, 'very busy', excused himself. Molesworth's parting shot was sorrowful but dignified.

> I shd have liked to tell you in person that I shall never forget your kindness to me long ago, especially about my trying to write. I thought it might have interested you to hear how I have succeeded, and I shd. have liked to show you my children. They and my books have made my life very different from what it wd. otherwise have been to me. Please forgive me for troubling you.[33]

She had triumphed in a more rewarding source of comfort and keep than her marriage. 'Major Molesworth had no idea of money,' said Ranald Paton, a family friend.[34] Molesworth's youngest sister announced, if she had married Richard they would probably have been happy and 'gone bust' together.[35] Such flippancy was not for serious, punctilious Molesworth. She now began to publish several books, stories and articles a year, careful to keep her copyright, playing off her eighteen publishers against each other to increase her pay, writing long after she said she was too old to pen more, wanting to 'sell well, even after I am dead', anything to secure income. She was always anxious about money. The ardent girl hammered herself into a concerned, business-like provider. 'I may tell you privately that I look forward to giving up all writing except my red Xmas book before long,' she told Mr Craik, her publisher at Macmillan. 'But I cannot as yet do this for I can only meet Lionel's Oxford education by writing more than this.'[36] In fact she never gave up any writing until extreme old age. The red book was her annual commitment to Macmillan, a children's story produced in a decorative red and black binding. When Lionel died aged 43 in 1917, she told her publisher, 'it cannot but add to my own responsibilities as I cannot but wish to do all I can for my daughter-in-law and [grand]children'.[37] She lived prudently, 'budgeting carefully all her expenses, otherwise I do not think they could have lived in the style they did', said a cousin, Gwen Molesworth.[38] Her books illustrate genteel excursions around poverty; in *Marrying and Giving in Marriage* (1887) Lady Christina, a mother dining alone with her daughter, announces, 'You needn't cut that tart, Aveline, it will come in so well cold for luncheon tomorrow.'[39] Poor gentry children in *Sweet Content*, unable to afford winter jackets, wear knitted vests under smart summer jackets.

Molesworth's life ricocheted with loss. Her elder son, Bevil, died aged 27 in 1898 in Patagonia. Seven years on, she told a just-bereaved friend: 'the bitter, bitter grief will often seem unbearable. Oh, how awfully well I know it – my boy's death seems as terrible as if it had only just happened.'[40] Indomitably through the tragedies, she worked on.

Anxiety swallowed up her middle years. Her family remembered her as 'a strict, even a stern mamma...it was many years before the sweetness came back'.[41] 'Her manner was distant and one worshipped from afar,' said a cousin who 'could not imagine her romping on the floor with small children'.[42] Never demonstrative, Molesworth showed her feelings stealthily; for instance, as children, Bevil and Lionel hated wearing new suits but were cheered by the sixpence they always found in a pocket. It was years before they realized their mother had put it there, not the tailor.

Her sons' adolescence worried her, and her reaction, as ever, was control. She 'kept her boys with too tight an eye', criticized a Molesworth cousin. When Bevil was seventeen she installed him in the City. 'I have done my utmost to get this chance for him; when he is older he will understand that such things are not easy,' she told Mr Craik.[43] 'Here's Mrs Molesworth Bevelling again,' commented Mrs Craik.[44] But Bevil opted for the freedom of a Patagonian ranch instead, a 'horrible wrench' Molesworth confessed. 'I did not think such a great trial was before me – I suppose one's whole life must be discipline of one kind or another.'[45] She urged the same self-discipline on her fictional child characters.

She returned to England in 1884 to Lexham Gardens, an unfashionable street in Kensington.[46] She lamented to Mr Craik, a firm friend who refused to make so long a journey: 'I wish you did not feel this so far out and I wish we were further in.'[47] Location mattered. Cabs were hard to find here, and Molesworth, who could not afford a carriage, found Kensington 'so gloomy and out-of the-way'.[48] In 1890 she moved slightly upmarket to 19 Sumner Place, and in 1899 finally settled with her youngest unmarried daughter Olive in a flat in fashionable Sloane Street.

Gradually Molesworth's innate charm ousted her outward severity. She had a talent for friendship and a weakness for the distinguished that was reflected in the titled protagonists of her children's books. Her literary renown helped her make interesting friends. The poet Swinburne wrote a eulogistic article just as she returned to England: 'since the death of George Eliot there is none left whose touch is so exquisite and masterly...as Mrs Molesworth's in depicting children'.[49] Swinburne, recovered from his alcoholic and other excesses, now idolized childhood. His visits to Molesworth were a compliment; he seldom left The Pines, his house in Putney. Rudyard Kipling, who said of *The Cuckoo Clock* 'much even now I know by heart';[50] Thackeray's daughter, Anne Thackeray Ritchie; the poet Jean Ingelow; the novelist Mrs Humphrey Ward – all became part of Molesworth's life. Another friend was Adrian Hope, secretary of Great Ormond Street Hospital, for which Molesworth did fund-raising work. His letters to his fiancée, Laura Troubridge, show a warm, vivacious Molesworth: 'The Molesworth dinner last night was amusing. All young people, no chaperones at all';[51] 'Mrs Molesworth urged me to throw everything to the winds and marry you at once'.[52] This couple were hard up, and Molesworth asked Laura, an artist, to illustrate her book *The Old Pincushion* (1889). She liked helping those she was fond of. Nothing was allowed to interfere with work, however. She wrote every morning and discouraged callers.

Her family brought immense pleasure. Olive, unmarried, adored her mother and never left her. 'A more dearly loved grandmother never lived,' said one granddaughter. Another remembered saying:

> 'Granny, in all the years we have been down Sloane Street we have never seen you leaning out of the window.' 'Ladies never lean out of windows.' 'But Granny if they had to see something.' 'They would put on their bonnets and go out and see.'[53]

Behaviour never ceased to matter.

Molesworth died a paradigm of Victorian endeavour and reward. Her funeral merited a headline in the *Sunday Times*: 'the well-known authoress, widow of the late Major Richard Molesworth...at Holy Trinity, Sloane Street...many literary friends attended'.[54] She had achieved her aims: social and literary status, well-kept secrets, a happy, united family. Success made her softer though never less self-disciplined. When Richard died in 1900 she felt she should remember him more generously. Mr Craik, one of the few who knew that she was only now really a widow, wrote on his death. Molesworth, glad to be frank to 'you, who know the whole', confided, 'I shall feel grateful to God if from now I can think of [him] with all the bitterness of disappointment and weary anxiety, taken away. For surely there was a great mingling of excuse for the faults &

follies that fell so heavily on those connected with him.'[55] This forgiving mood was inspired by 'dear, loyal-hearted' Bevil, dead now for three years but still 'ever present'.

Molesworth had penned her guidelines years before in a children's novel, *Grandmother Dear* (1876). The grandmother, unnecessarily angry with her granddaughter and now sorry, declares:

> I hope that up to the very last of my life I shall have lessons to learn....Or rather I should say that I shall be able to learn them. To these lessons there is no limit.[56]

This spur to self-improvement Molesworth, disillusioned but always determined, upheld not only in the easy way, making her characters utter noble platitudes, but in a harder way, in the conduct of her own life.

THE OPEN BOOK

Molesworth's books elicited a varied response. One critic applauded her tolerance. 'Mrs Molesworth shows how by being too strict, parents may destroy all that is best in a child's character.'[57] Another deplored an 'undue importance attached to childish faults'.[58] *The Westminster Budget*, an upmarket intellectual review, found her characters 'all natural, possible human beings'.[59] Her urgent concern with upbringing and her employment of realism make her a prime source of contemporary values. A fantasy and domestic tale will illustrate her achievement.

The Cuckoo Clock (1877) tells of motherless Griselda, who leaves her father overseas to live with two elderly aunts. Bored, cross and lonely, she is befriended by a magical cuckoo from a clock, a querulous character, precursor of Nesbit's Psammead, who takes her on adventures and finally produces a friend for her, Phil. *The Cuckoo Clock*, recently reprinted, has seldom been out of print, due to its charm and perennially appealing fantastical boundaries. Critics see it as a *Bildungsroman*, a novel of youth leading its protagonist to morality and maturity.[60] Also, it both promulgates and curtails the principles of upbringing and education that Molesworth expected of a child of Griselda's age, sex and class. Griselda, the cuckoo tells her frequently, has 'a great deal to learn', though 'there are a great many things you're not intended to know'. Femininity and youth, Molesworth taught, constituted a bar to knowledge.

Molesworth understands but will not allow rebelliousness. Griselda, furious at her aunt's description of the clock's punctuality – 'Good little cuckoo. What an example he sets you. His life is spent in the faithful discharge of duty' – hurls a book at him. She is 'Impatient Griselda'. Chaucer's medieval Griselda, innocent of her accusations, is abject, and submits. Victorian Griselda, unlike her namesake, is spirited but finally acquires submission. Both Griseldas represent restrictive female plight, though Molesworth finds space within girlhood boundaries for creativity.

The book begins:

> Once upon a time in an old town, in an old street, there stood a very old house. Such a house as you could hardly find nowadays, however you searched, for it belonged to a gone-by time – a time now quite passed away.

The rhythmical incantation poses themes of time, enchantment and interiority. The book begins in wintertime, keeping Griselda inside. The cuckoo takes Griselda deep inside the house, into the cuckoo clock, inside the Chinese cabinet's endless alcoves which magically expand into a Mandarin palace, and in her own room, where he creates living pictures of her family history. Excursions into fantasy satisfy Griselda's craving for fun while informing her that creativity lies within the self. Amusement laced with instruction was a staple of Victorian children's literature. Molesworth's books teach her readers moral self-searching. Frequently in her texts heroines experience revelations of self-knowledge as they probe labyrinthine domestic interiors. Molesworth uses the house as a metaphor of female self-exploration within the dictates of the feminine domain. Her ideal female self consists of behavioural self-control and imaginative power – in other words, limitless exploration of the mind contained by domesticity.

A visit to beautiful Butterfly Land, mistaken by Griselda for fairyland, shows her the satisfaction of duty, obedience and industriousness. The butterflies are not playing, as Griselda imagined, but busy propagating flowers, obeying orders, as everything must, she learns, to avoid chaos. 'There's the sun now, just getting up, and the moon going to bed – they are always obeying, aren't they?' School lessons, which she had found tiresome, become quick and pleasurable under this approach, as does her relationship with her pernickety aunts. She never understands, indeed is not meant to, her last adventure to the eerie dead sea on the other side of the moon – Molesworth's metaphor for nihilism – but hopes eternally to find fairyland – Molesworth's vaguely Christian metaphor for spiritual joy. There are doors to it in the house, the cuckoo tells her, and she finally learns that she must find her own way there – a lesson, hammered home, of spiritual searching and fulfilment within domesticity.

Griselda learns order: social order (a devoted servant props up the class system), and moral order (Griselda acquires girlhood virtues). Generational order shows her the reassuring legacy of family history: the cuckoo's beautiful 'pictures from the past' cure her disgust at her likeness to her dead grandmother. Nature's seasonal order brings growth and fecundity: when spring arrives, she meets Phil, who, much younger, arouses her motherliness, the sum of all the self-knowledge she has acquired, thus allowing her cuckoo guide to leave her. Her bursts of rebellion have been subverted by flights into healing imaginative consciousness, converting her via submissiveness to motherliness, the goal of Victorian girlhood.

There was little other choice. Female career options were limited as the turn of the century saw the 'angel in the house' chafe to become the New Woman. Mitchell argues cogently that the same period saw, as never before, the emergence of girlhood as a separate culture. The girlhood phenomenon, evidenced in an explosion of girl-orientated magazines, sports, clubs and schools, developed from changes in child labour laws and education.[61] New opportunities, however, were subjected to scrutiny. An 1895 study showed that university-educated women were more likely to become teachers than wives,[62] proof that too much education turned wife-potential into bluestocking sterility.

Molesworth herself was wary of female cleverness. In a fairy story in which the best girl will inherit a magic spinning wheel, the most deserving is not clever Bertha, who wants to earn enough as a seamstress to pay for schooling to become a teacher, but selfless Amanda, who wants to make warm clothes for the poor (*The Magic Spinning Wheel* 1890). The pursuit of learning appears to be another form of selfishness. The Victorians anyway considered female natural ability to be a health risk. The precocity of Molesworth's daughter Violet had frightened her. 'I made her not learn much and I talked nonsense with her.'[63] Molesworth was not opposed to female education and employment; she tried, for instance, to help a friend's Cambridge-educated daughter who 'has nothing to do...wishes to put her education to good use...and live in London' to find a secretarial job.[64] Her books, however, told a different, safer story. Here she advocated not her own example as family provider, or even her literary success, but a conventional path leading to marriage, her apogee, and motherhood, its peak. She pushed her girl readers towards a marital dependency, like Victoria, the world's most powerful queen and empress, who still claimed 'being married gives one one's position which nothing else can'.[65]

Nevertheless, the emergence of a new demanding breed of girl led Molesworth to re-examine girlhood itself. 'Who am I?' is the theme of *Sheila's Mystery* (1895) her most angst-packed book for girls. Sheila, aged 12, despite a beautiful home and loving parents, is unhappy. Her horrible jealous temper flares, based on the fear that she is ugly, unlovable, unloved and adopted – common adolescent convictions all. Her younger sister Honor, whose first name is also Sheila, is sweet, fair and pretty, safely ensconced in the security of untroubled little girlhood. Their shared name makes them like mirror twins, combining the dark fears that lurk behind bright childhood with the erratic nature of the child/adolescent divide. One night Sheila overhears her parents talking secrets, discovers they really did adopt a daughter, and runs away, feeling justified in jettisoning her family.

Now isolated from her familial identity, she takes on another name and tries but fails to re-establish herself. She misses her family too much. Led by gypsies to a humble farming family who, in the best coincidences of fiction, appear to be her nearest relations, she still feels an unhappy outcast. She solves her lonely predicament with self-control, overcoming her anger to become lovable at last. She realizes her unhappiness stemmed from selfishly dwelling overmuch on self. Now her parents return to reclaim her, telling her Honor, not Sheila, is the adopted daughter, the farmers' relation. Having discovered Sheila's whereabouts, her parents had decided to leave her at the farm in order to cure her of her faults.

The subtext seethes with the Victorian fascination with money, class, behaviour and secrets. Sheila's parents had adopted Honor, an orphan heiress, and kept it quiet to oblige her dying well-born grandfather, distressed that his son had married beneath him. He wanted Honor removed from her mother's family, convinced they had designs on his fortune. *Sheila's Mystery* is a harsh, emotional book, reflecting ruthless sanctions considered perfectly appropriate.

Molesworth's concentration on Sheila's despair has a deeper implication, however. The unhappy-girl theme runs frequently through her child novels. In *Rosy* (1882) the 8-year-old heroine is jealous as the family re-forms when her unfamiliar parents return from India with a new baby and unknown elder brother. In *The Carved Lions* (1895) Geraldine's misery when her parents leave her to go abroad to recoup their fortune stupefies her. In *Sweet Content* (1891) Connie resents the implications of her position as the only surviving child of the family. The dysfunctional family, disrupted by death, economic swings and the demands of the empire, was a middle-class social norm. But Molesworth sees its crises always through the cry of a daughter, not a son.

Molesworth's angry heroines reflect a disquiet underlying middle-class girlhood. Its constraints of class and paucity of fulfilment other than marriage, at a time when censuses show a growing number of 'surplus' single women, created a sense of unease. Molesworth's heroines feel unloved and undervalued. In dwelling on the rebel-phenomenon, Molesworth underlines her significance. But each heroine's struggle results in a self-knowledge that condemns her insurrection as 'selfishness'. Individuality, painfully drawn, is hammered into submission as self is subsumed. Molesworth is poised between empathy and a loud trumpet call to a stiff upper lip and self-denial.

There existed already in girls' literature a tradition of self-improvement. Molesworth as a girl had revered Charlotte Yonge who, as Yonge's biographer said, made 'trying to be very good...interesting and romantic to thousands of girls'.[66] But the apotheosis, the Victorian 'angel' image, reinforced by definition in discourses such as medicine, psychiatry, law and education,[67] was always an impossible one for women to live up to. If the shrine was a mirage, then cracks in the edifice were inevitable. Spirited heroines like Jane Eyre and Maggie Tulliver heralded a refusal to conform to expectations. Reynolds and Humble point to a late nineteenth-century literary appreciation of the rebel for her own sake.[68] Molesworth, however, had a tensely balanced approach. The rebelliousness of her child heroines shows their difficulty in learning to wear the mask demanded by a culture that divided feeling from behaviour. Their individuality is expressed but denied; their rage identified but unacceptable. She hears but silences her heroines' scream for appreciation.

Molesworth creates a physical sense of femality. Her child heroines dress, undress, tussle with untidy streaming hair, stamp, pout, cry, hug, kiss, and eat hungrily. Their energy and sensuality, lurking in the subtext, are, like their mental flare-ups, firmly subdued as they conform to controlled young ladyhood. Molesworth acknowledges and stamps down the rampant beast within. Unsurprisingly parents and critics considered Molesworth a safe writer for girls, while she touched a raw nerve in female identity. Her readers could dwell, as did her texts, on feeling. Her tropes in *Sheila's Mystery* of being unloved, an outcast, victim of misunderstandings, of being ugly, could elicit a warm emotional response of adolescent identification, while the reconciliation closure adds momentum to the happy family dream. 'The reader weeps because her own family is not so warm and close as the culture tells her families are; the ideal may seldom exist, but the overwhelming ideological pretense makes girls ache for what they are 'missing'.[69] If the happy family is hard to maintain in reality, Molesworth's realistic fictionalization of its difficulties, followed by her unrealistic fairy-tale-like happy resolutions, presents it equally and contradictorily as both desirable and illusory.

Molesworth liked a realistic style. Her insertion in her fiction of the authorial 'I', as in 'I am telling you the story of a real little girl and boy' (*Carrots*) posits her truthfulness on her readers.

Even though this truthfulness is itself fiction, it was supported by her realist approach to her characters: 'I live with them...I listen to what they talk about. I feel them becoming very real.'[70] Her realism was further supported by her aim of moral improvement. 'She understands [her readers'] wants, she desires to help them,' approved Salmon, a noted contemporary critic.[71] Even her fairy tales resound with her rallying cry to good behaviour. These also have a realist base. Molesworth was adamant all 'children's stories should be real', demanding, 'Is true fairyland unreal?'[72]

Molesworth's magical heroines are clever princesses, armed with wit, skill and courage, who reach beyond their parents to conduct and conclude events. Their mothers try unsuccessfully to restrain them, dreading the cruel world's blows. Their fathers are feeble. It is tempting to see in her princesses strong, careful, compassionate women emerging from their shackles – Molesworth's ideal female vision. As Zipes points out, fairy-tale writers use fantastic projections in a liberating manner.[73] Molesworth's magic heroines reiterate her vision of the only possible excursion outside convention that she felt women could attain – imaginative creativity, the secret of her own achievement. Her fairy tales, unlike her domestic tales, promote feminist success, but set it in never-never land, a place equally of impossibility and desire. Molesworth's thinking is always torn between poles.

In *The Story of a King's Daughter* the handsome lover, Prince Halbert, possessor of a filthy temper, is punished by transformation into a hideous monster. Courageous Princess Auréole's love magically restores his looks and reforms his nature. Molesworth, when young and optimistic, hoped in vain to help her husband's temper and their marriage with love. Only in fairy tales did she allow that love alone could realize wishes. Real life, she knew, hurled brickbats. She never stopped preparing her readers for setbacks. 'We want to brace, not to discourage; to make our readers thoughtful.'[74] Molesworth saw her world as a dangerous, slippery place. Her books are a plea for constant watchfulness; she knew only moral endeavour and self-control could keep society steady, its families safe, its daughters aiming at middle-class respectability.

4

Frances Hodgson Burnett

I am living in a fairy story.

(*A Little Princess*, 1905)

Frances Hodgson Burnett, author of fifty-six books and thirteen plays, is now chiefly remembered for three children's books, *Little Lord Fauntleroy*, *A Little Princess*, and *The Secret Garden*. These, constantly reissued as films and television programmes, have never been out of print, and have become a yardstick in children's literature criticism. Grounded in realism, they take mythic form as they soar into a fairy-tale idealism. Their huge popularity and continual capacity for analysis pushes Burnett into a seminal position. Something in these books crystallized their age at the moment of publication, while they continually appeal to the present with more grist than mere nostalgia. New insight into both her books and her age is harvested from each succeeding generation, as psychological, historical and cultural interpretations change. Frances Hodgson Burnett is a classic in the canon of children's literature.

Burnett was a better judge of character in her books than of the people in her life. Her tragedy was the gap between her utopian dreams and the unhappy reality she made for herself. Her two marriages made her miserable. Eager to make as much money as possible, her constant Atlantic crossings (thirty-three times in all) enhanced her literary output and publicity but meant she saw little of her children as they grew older. She was racked with guilt when Lionel, the elder, died of consumption aged 16. Divorced, separated, with two living husbands, the second ten years younger than herself, her situation was the stuff of bitterness and scandal. 'Women are not happy as a rule,' the benchmark voice pronounces in her adult novel *Through One Administration*.[1] On the other hand, she believed 'there ought to be a tremendous lot of natural, splendid happiness in the life of every human being'.[2] She converted her lofty convictions into the idealism of her books, a contrast, both, to the pitfalls in her life. A biographical approach to her work sheds light on how and why the chasm occurred.

IN THE REAL GARDEN? THE MAKING OF A STORY-TELLER

Burnett was born in Manchester in 1849, the third of five children of Edwin and Eliza Hodgson. Her father, a fairly well-to-do general furnishing ironmonger and silversmith, sold upmarket household goods. Burnett inherited her father's appreciation of the best money could buy. When her father died when she was 4, her mother continued the business herself. This was brave, as Mrs Hodgson was unbusiness-like and 'guileless', Burnett said, 'all unfit to contend with a harsh, sharp, sordid world'.[3] As income diminished, Mrs Hodgson moved her family to a smaller house in Islington Square, bordered by Manchester's rough backstreets, home to the poor who worked in the cotton mills nearby.

Frances, nicknamed Fannie, plump and red-haired, nevertheless grew up in a world of middle-class respectability. Until she was 15, when an uncle advised them to emigrate to America, she led an ordinary family life, cuddling the baby Edwina, close to her next sister Edith (a lifelong closeness), hiding her bursts of creativity from her teasing brothers, in the security of nightly prayers, school, best friends and heavy mahogany furniture.

It was never enough. At the eagerly anticipated parties she attended as a child, she wondered secretly, 'Is this *really* the Party?'[4] Real life was unconvincing and unsatisfying, but imagination transformed her commonplace world into something better, and led her to create a story world. Burnett preferred life enhanced as a story. When Sara Crewe says, 'Everything's a story. You are a story – I am a story',[5] Burnett expressed her own frame of mind.

At school, like Sara Crewe, she was the acknowledged story-teller, enthralling her classmates with the saga of Edith

Somerville, whose hair, eyes, figure and clothes were the subject of daily different clichés. 'Just tell a little Edith Somerville,' they begged, and she always began, '...and so...'[6] Story was ongoing. She never stopped. As an adult, she wove a fiction about herself as the 'Romantick Lady', as an ideal mother and fairy godmother. As Bixler points out, 'she spent so much imaginative energy on her public image that it became another of her fictions'.[7] The unrealistic and relentless idealism of her books constituted yet another. It represented her vision of happiness, which, though it never materialized in her life, she never stopped believing in because she felt it ought to exist.

The commonplace stagnated her. All her stories were distilled from realism hauled into an inspiring ideal. Her autobiography reveals the way her mind worked in *The One I Knew Best of All*, subtitled *A Memory of the Mind of a Child*. While she was at school, two fellow-pupils died. The first, Alfie, was dull, 'not clever, not pretty, not engaging', remarkable only for his bluish-purple lips. When he died, little Frances, eager to investigate death, found, when she went to see the body laid out, that Alfie remained unexciting. She could not imagine him as a glorious angel and felt only 'dreariness'. Not so when Selina died. She was beautiful, quaint, enchanting, the pet of the school, and only 3 years old. Frances found herself saying all day, 'Not Selina? Selina!' She saw Selina's bedroom hung with white, with white rosebuds everywhere 'like a little chapel of snow'; the child herself, bedecked with roses, looked even lovelier in death. Here at last was the ultimate example of beautiful child-death, and Frances felt tender and stirred and satisfied. The archetype child-without-parallel appears in all her most well-known children's books. Cedric Errol is the sunniest child in the world, Mary Lennox the most disagreeable, Sara Crewe the most imaginative.

Two childhood worlds on the edge of her own were early fodder for transforming prosaic everyday into story. She was fascinated by the poor backstreet children who passed Islington Square on their way to the mills, debating family fights, beatings, drunks, in a dialect that she adored and never forgot. In her Islington Square bedroom, some trick of the light flung onto the ceiling a reflection of the domestic goings-on of a backstreet couple who lived the house row behind. She gazed avidly. 'Ah, the charm of it! ... What they did when they moved out of the range of reflection, what they said to each other...were things to be excitedly guessed at.'[8]

She found similar inspiration in observing nature. She describes creeping through a door in a wall of the Square into the deserted garden of a house about to be demolished. Only docks and thistles grew there.

> If an older person could have looked on – understanding – surely he would have seen light and colour and glow come into her child's face.
> 'You are roses,' she said. 'You are violets – and lilies – and hyacinths and daffodils and snowdrops! You are!'[9]

She felt the same degree of intensity at 15 when her mother moved the family to America. Now in rural Tennessee, Frances watched the weather, birds and flowers in the woods, experiencing 'an exultation, beautiful and strange'. 'The blue violets seemed to rush out of the earth.'[10] This spiritual identification with nature was perhaps the genesis of the 'Magic' of The Secret Garden. With it was her instinctive need to transform and dramatize. She pretended she was 'a young, young Dryad, in these her Dryad days'.[11]

Her teenage pantheism foretells the mythological and pastoral undercurrents of The Secret Garden (see Bixler). The restorative friendship-in-nature that she gives to Mary, Colin and Dickon, however, contrasts with her own experience. The young Frances was a loner. No one looked on '– understanding –.'

A better financial life in America had failed to materialize. The Hodgsons were now extremely poor and often hungry. Frances, who had been privately scribbling love stories in a cold attic, wrapped in a shawl and hugging the cat for warmth, decided to help out by sending one to a ladies' magazine. She discovered that manuscripts would be unread unless they were written on foolscap paper, and sent with the correct postage. Unable to afford either paper or postage, she picked wild grapes to sell in the local market, and used the profits accordingly, informing the editor, 'my object is remuneration'. Not only did she get her fee; the editor asked for more. 'Gates of Paradise', she said, now flew open.

An age discrepancy lurks in Burnett's account of her launch

into writing. In her autobiography, and in an article in *The Lady's Realm* (1896), 'How I Served My Apprenticeship', Burnett says she was 15. In fact she was 18 when her first story, *'Hearts and Diamonds'*, appeared in *Godey's Magazine* in 1868. The images of the very young girl, poverty, the cold attic, the cat, the shawl, the wild grapes gathered for manuscript paper, followed by success and fame, are imbued with fairy-tale romance. Burnett combined ambition, talent, determination, enthusiasm and practicality with a compulsion to reinterpret prosaic reality into a better story.

Perhaps this optimistic outlook lured her into matrimony. Swan Burnett was the doctor's son in Tennessee, clever, small, with a limp. Frances advised him what books to read. Their courtship lasted seven years. After agreeing to marry him, Frances, by this time writing for nearly every magazine in America and earning well, disappeared to England for a year. 'I cannot weave silk if I see nothing but calico – calico – calico', she told him.[12] The bait of new material for her books was evidently greater than Swan's attractions. However, the mellowing combination of his absence and his letters finally drew her to marriage on her return in 1873, though she was still in no hurry. Her wedding dress was not finished, and she wanted to wait for it.

They were incompatible. Swan's career, the study of the eye, explored facts. Frances dealt in sweeps of the imagination. Swan liked cosy little houses; Frances wanted to be stimulated with luxury, travel and interesting people. Confident and independent, she enjoyed control. 'Somehow I felt quite sure that if I could do anything I must do it myself, and I could live on what I earned if I worked hard enough.'[13] Soon she turned the conventional marriage set-up back to front, supporting herself, Swan, whose training she paid for in Paris, and her two boys.

She wrote and wrote, though she was often ill. She suffered frequently from depression. A private poem, written four weeks before her second child's birth, is pregnant with resentment of Swan.

> When I am dead & lie before you low
> With folded hands & cheek & lip of snow,
> As you stand downward
> Will you know
> Why the end came & why I wearied so?[14]

'Her favourite image of herself was that of a fairy godmother, and the power as well as the magnanimity of that role must have appealed to her.'[15] Her novels frequently refer to the pleasure of money. Keyser suggests that Mary's part in *The Secret Garden*, forefronted, then seconded, with Colin's recovery, reflects Burnett's ambivalence towards self-assertive females like herself. 'She tried to rationalise her writing as unselfish service and when she could not ignore its self-assertive and self-serving role, punished herself with ill-health.'[16] Her ambitions, however, were high. 'I want my chestnuts off a higher bough,' she told her sister at this time.[17]

Meanwhile, she developed her stories from light romance featuring fortune reversals to tales of Lancashire pit workers, peaking in *That Lass O'Lowrie's* (1877), her first best-seller, which earned her comparison with George Eliot. Although so young when she left Manchester, its nuances and cadences had lodged in her excellent memory. The powerful story of Joan Lowrie, the pit girl, who marries Derrick, the gentleman engineer, was inspired by a childhood memory of a majestic, ragged girl from the Islington Square backstreets. The plot is innovative and subversive. Pillars of society are upended. Derrick prefers rough Joan to gentle Anice, the self-satisfied vicar's daughter. Joan will learn to be a lady. As Laski says, 'for most Victorian writers such a position could have been resolved only by the death of one of the lovers'.[18] Burnett's standard theme of realism soaring to fairy-tale transformation of fortune relates to her own rags-to-riches determination to achieve economic security. The book links her appreciation of the classless opportunities offered by the New World with the traditions of the Old.

That Lass O'Lowrie's was followed by a succession of lucrative pot-boilers. It is tempting to read into her next book, *Through One Administration* (1883) Burnett's feelings about her marriage. This book, a best-seller, centres on Washington's political intrigues and the unhappy marriage of Bertha and Richard Amory. Reviews compared Burnett favourably with Henry James. Burnett's son Vivian described Bertha's situation as 'entirely fictitious...[though] the manner in which she expressed herself about it was very much the Frances Hodgson Burnett of 1880', and admits she gave Richard 'certain physical characteristics' of her husband.[19] Richard is slight, lithe, delicate, with an 'almost feminine' beauty. Bertha's father, the authorial voice, sums up her predicament.

> He was picturesque and pathetic – and poetic...Of course his picturesque magnanimity told...reaction set in, and she began to feel the fascination of making him happy.[20]

Burnett had a soft heart for male physical weakness. Her sister wrote of Swan and his limp, 'Fannie, with her tenderness for any sort of disability or disadvantage, well, knowing Fannie, can't you see how it inevitably came about?'[21] *Through One Administration* highlights the nineteenth-century female conflict. Bertha knows she is cleverer than women are supposed to be, and in order to succeed as Richard's wife, develops a falsely frivolous character. Similarly, Burnett presented a public image of romantic femininity that hid her 'unfeminine' drive. Though Bertha enjoys power she comes to grief as she allows her husband to manipulate her. Bertha is a complex character, a 'poor child' who needs protection, dominating, maternal, and a poor judge of herself, while she also valiantly and unhappily upholds female convention. Bertha's story reveals Burnett's frame of mind. Bixler comments

> An awareness of how Burnett aggressively pursued her career and her non-conformist lifestyle under the cover of an ultra feminine public exterior points to a similar strategy in much of her popular fiction, while allaying readers' anxieties about changing roles for women by adhering to the love story formula with its happy ending in a happy marriage.[22]

The Ruskin-like perception of desirable femininity forced the façade behind which Burnett formed her outlook and presented her image. *Through One Administration* ends unhappily, touching a raw nerve Burnett never repeated. Elsewhere the unlikeliness of her romantic closures both supports and indicts the mores that created them. Within the façade of femininity lies another Victorian obliqueness in which meaning is hidden behind a curtain. Burnett's constant fiction of a fairy-tale-like happy ending underlines the reality of improbability of fulfilment for clever women.

'Maternal instinct', Bertha's father comments, is 'a great safeguard where life is not satisfactory'. Burnett herself often said, 'The one perfect thing in my life was the childhood of my boys.'[23] Lionel was born a year after her marriage, and Vivian eighteen months later. She delighted in Lionel's filthy toddler exploits; 'the roughest, biggest, tearingest rascal the family had ever known...the most engaging little sinner out', she called him.[24] She also seems to have relished the role of tactile mothering. Vivian as a baby had a habit of cuddling her while asleep, 'making a heavenly downy necklace of both his arms'. She loved disentangling his hair while telling him stories. As a child, his politeness to rich and poor alike, and staunch, republican ardour amused and impressed her. He also made her feel treasured. He watched over her when she was ill, brought her flowers, left love tokens. As she said, 'there is nothing so loving as a child who is loved'. Vivian's reassurance filled a void. 'Where did he learn – faithful and tender heart – to be such a lover as he was? Surely no woman ever had such a lover before!'[25] Vivian combined, to Burnett's delight, the roles of loving child and adult cavalier. Burnett found her child's love easier to respond to than any other.

Little Lord Fauntleroy was published in 1886, when Vivian was 10. Burnett had her brainwave when Vivian wondered what a duke was.

'I will write a story about him,' I said. How shall I bring a small American boy into close relationship with an English nobleman – irascible, conservative, disagreeable? Eureka! Son of younger son, separated from ill-tempered noble father because he has married a poor young American beauty. Young father dead, elder brothers dead, boy comes into title! Vivian shall be he – just Vivian with his curls and his eyes and his friendly, kind little soul. Little Lord Something-or-other. What a pretty title. Little Lord – what?

And a day later it was Little Lord Fauntleroy. A story like that is easily written. In part it was being lived before my eyes.[26]

Burnett had purified realism into an acme of escapist perfection. Furthermore, the idealized Vivian gave her, as never before, wealth and fame. The book became a best-seller on both sides of the Atlantic. A contemporary reviewer thought it would have as much impact as *Jane Eyre*. It was turned into a play, first produced in London, not by her pen and without her permission. She quickly wrote her own very successful *The Real Little Lord Fauntleroy*, sued the playwright, and won her case, thus prompting the Copyright Act of 1911. In gratitude, well-known writers gave her a diamond bracelet. It was said that *Little Lord Fauntleroy* had improved Anglo-American relations. The prime minister, Gladstone, asked to meet her. No wonder that her children's childhood was her 'one perfect thing', in itself and in its spin-offs. As well as the child-redeemer/irascible old sinner relationship, the book celebrates mother/child bonds, and concludes with widowed Mrs Errol nestling in the earl's fatherly protection. Burnett hardly remembered her own father. Orphaned before her marriage and self-appointed provider, she presents Mrs Errol's celibate, maternal, child-like dependency as a nirvana. Many of her children's books culminate in the restoration of a child to a parent figure, though it is impossible to know whether Burnett drew on her own longings or the props of a good plot.

Seizing on her success, Burnett wrote nine children's books in the next ten years, as well as five adult books. Of the better-known books, *Sara Crewe* (1888, the first version of the more famous 1905 *A Little Princess*), *Editha's Burglar* (1888), *Little Saint Elizabeth* (1890), *Two Little Pilgrims' Progress* (1895) are all remarkable for the magical conversions effected by powerfully innocent, determined child protagonists on their circumstances and their elders. All are as unlikely and idealistic as fairy stories. Editha softens the heart of the burglar robbing her home when she asks him to be quiet so as not to waken her mamma. In the end he gives her his own silver watch. Elizabeth is protected by her innocence as she tries to donate her fabulous wealth to the aggressive poor of New York. Robin and Meg, orphans aiming at betterment, run away to the Chicago World Fair, where they magnetize a rich disillusioned widower who adopts them happily ever after. Burnett concluded *Two Little Pilgrims' Progress* with her belief in idealism trumping grim reality.

> Fairy stories are happening every day. There are beautiful things happening in the world; there are many people with kind and generous hearts...giving what is theirs to give, and being glad in the giving – and Spring comes every year. These make fairy stories.[27]

Her fairy-tale genre, soaked in realism, could be read either as a comforting dream or actually possible in a self-help effort as exhorted by Samuel Smiles's best-seller tome *Self-Help*. Her wish-fulfilment stories echoed the opportunities offered by the industrial revolution, America's classless society and sheer determination.

Burnett became increasingly restless. Based in America, she constantly crossed the Atlantic, taking houses in England every year, fitting in sojourns in Europe. It was

> the simplest affair in the world to drive down to the wharves and take a steamer which landed one after a more or less interesting voyage in Liverpool. From there one went to London, or Paris, or Rome, but first or last it always led the traveller to the treading of green, velvet English turf.[28]

Travel at this time was more arduous than this suggests, but Burnett's zest dismissed the trouble for the gains. Her dual need for America ('America. It doesn't stand still. It goes and gets what it wants')[29] and the peace she felt England offered reflects her conflicting cravings: hungry, have-it-all, mystic, reflective. Burnett travelled with a lady companion-secretary, for convenience and propriety, while the boys mostly stayed with their father. Finally, in 1898 she divorced Swan, telling Vivian, 'to be neither married nor unmarried is a difficult position'.[30] Swan's desertion was given as the legal cause of their divorce, though Burnett's own absences from home were more apparent.

Burnett now put herself into a more tricky position. In London in 1889 (she took a house in Lexham Gardens in that year) she met Stephen Townsend, ten years younger than herself, like Swan a doctor, son of a vicar, and actor manqué. She hoped to propel him into a glittering acting career. They married in 1900, when Burnett was 50. For the second time Burnett's marriage began with nurturing and ended in disaster. Stephen was at first irresistibly attractive to Burnett. He supported her when she was ill and helped her when she tore around Europe in 1890 with her son Lionel, desperately seeking a cure for his fatal consumption. Since Stephen was a doctor, his presence was not scandalous, and if they were lovers, as Thwaite argues convincingly, the irregularity was thus concealed.

She regretted it almost instantly. She told her sister Edith, 'He talks about my 'duties as a wife' as if I had married him of my own accord – as if I had not been forced and blackguarded and blackmailed into it.'[31] Burnett told Vivian, 'Understand that when I say your father never assumed a single responsibility of manhood, I know another who has assumed even fewer and done more evil';[32] 'It is all so grotesquely hideous – it is like some wild nightmare'.[33] Burnett's biographers unanimously conclude he blackmailed her into marriage, threatening revelations of their irregular past, because he wanted her money and parts in her plays, and that he abused her during the marriage. 'Could you have believed that I could ever hate a creature and wish him ill?', she wrote to Vivian, 'What I have to struggle with now are these surging waves of awful hate which sweep over me They are not like me'.[34] In 1902, Burnett, in a state of collapse, told him the marriage was over. Thwaite thinks it likely she bought him off.

She dealt with the 'awful hate' by concentrating on her creed of positive thinking. 'We never discuss painful things – that is our religion, our philosophy.'[35] She annexed the Victorian attitude of drawing a veil over the unsavoury to her natural instinct to rise above it. A galaxy of interesting friendships helped. She knew Henry James, Israel Zangwell, and Bernard Berenson. Another resource was Maytham Hall in Kent, which she had rented on a long lease in 1898. Its eighteen bedrooms, two entrance lodges, outbuildings and walled garden made it a quintessence of English upper-class country charm. Here she entertained, gardened and generously looked after the villagers. She was the lady of the manor, a role she enjoyed as to the manner born. She always found a sort of peace in giving. After Lionel died, she had endowed a bed in his name in a London nursing home for waif children, and set up a Reading Room in a club for poor boys, to which she gave all his books.

Five years after Stephen's departure Burnett published an adult novel about an unhappy, violent marriage which it is impossible not to connect with her own. In *The Shuttle* (1907) cruel, sadistic Sir Nigel Anstruthers, who owns a huge crumbling mansion, marries Rosalie, a young American heiress, for her fortune. Burnett had told a friend in 1900 that Stephen dwelt on 'the impropriety of a woman *not* handing over her fortune to her husband'.[36] Nigel subjects Rosalie to mental and physical abuse until she gives him her money, whereupon he scarpers abroad with a mistress while she grows haggard and ugly. Rosalie's sister Betty arrives from America determined to save her and her hunchback son. Betty and Rosalie are mirror images. Betty is strong-minded, practical and generous; Rosalie is vulnerable. Betty triumphs. Armed with money and determination, she repairs the house, transforms the gardens, restores Rosalie's looks, outwits Nigel who tries to rape her, and destroys him with a telepathic call for help.

The Shuttle's themes were close to Burnett's heart and foreshadow *The Secret Garden* (1911). *The Shuttle* was written in her lovingly made walled rose garden at Maytham Hall; *The Secret Garden*, written in America when Maytham Hall had been sold, nostalgically recalls it. Both feature an ill boy, a hunchback, a robin, an abandoned house with endless rooms, the restoration of a garden, will-power, clairvoyance and a veneration of nature. Betty says,

> Once I sat for quite a long time before a rose, watching it. When I saw it begin to listen...I seemed to be so strangely near such a strange thing. It was Life – Life coming back in answer to what we cannot hear.[37]

This passage exults in the same way as the teenage Burnett who watched violets 'rush out of the earth' in Tennessee, and Colin who cried, 'I shall live forever and ever and ever!' as 'the sun fell warm upon his face like a hand with a lovely touch'[38] when he first saw the secret garden.

The lengthy *Shuttle* took a long time to write. During its gestation *The Making of a Marchioness* (1901) burst from Burnett in two weeks. This Cinderella story of poor, virtuous Emily Fox-Seton, who beats off all contenders rejoicing in better lineage, wealth, brains and sex appeal, to win Lord Walderhurst, the catch of the Season, has been considered her best adult book. She herself loved it. 'The cleverness of the thing (I know it is clever) lies in the way in which the most wildly romantic situation is made compatible with perfectly everyday and unromantic people and things.' Once again Burnett tweaked an unremarkable setting into a fairy-story closure.

'It is', Laski points out, 'far more than Mrs Hodgson Burnett could have realised, a cruel revelation of the nature of Edwardian society.'[39] All the women except unassuming Emily are desperate to marry to avoid public condemnation as spinster-failures. It is also a commentary on the unsatisfactory nature of Edwardian marriage. 'Husbands and wives annoy each other very little these days,' says cynical old Lady Maria,[40] by whose auspices Emily meets the marquis. If they behave 'within the limits of decorum', it is implied, if conventional discretion is observed, husband and wife can lead separate lives. The marriages analysed in the book are deficient. Alec Osborn, Lord Walderhurst's heir, manipulates his wife and beats her up. Emily's devotion to Walderhurst, disparaged as 'early Victorian', means that she fails to tell him that Alec, who wants to remain the heir, is trying to murder her. She doesn't want to upset Walderhurst. Unromantic Walderhurst, middle-aged, with a poor digestion, is frank. 'I am a selfish man and I want an unselfish woman.'[41] He is finally transformed into a fairy-tale hero when he recalls Emily from the brink of death by sheer will.

Burnett's life creed was will-power. In *The White People* (1917) she reveals her beliefs. Dedicated to Lionel, it is the story of Ysabel, who can see ghosts – the white people. Ysabel loves fatally ill Hector, while Hector's adored mother dreads his death. Hector is a famous author, a genius of extraordinary wisdom whom Bixler identifies with George MacDonald, whom Burnett had met on a lecture tour. In Burnett's *The Closed Room* (1905) the heroine, Judith, is, like MacDonald's Diamond in *At the Back of the North Wind* (1871), the child of poor artisans and, like Diamond and Hector in *The White People,* 'falls awake' in another more beautiful land.

Ysabel comforts Hector and his mother not with conventional religion, but with her knowledge that the dead still surround the living with love; that death is pure rapture and means 'awakening free'. When Hector dies, Ysabel lives with Hector's mother. Burnett suggests that Ysabel is now safe; her love, unconsummated, is pure. Love and marriage, she implies, are ill-fated; life carries terrible chains: earthly strength comes from the parent–child relationship, leaving ecstasy, the gift of death, to come. Burnett's dedicatory poem to Lionel shows how, seventeen years later, she refuses to let death take him away. Natural laws appear impotent in the face of Burnett's will.

> The stars come nightly to the sky
> The tidal wave unto the sea;
> Nor time, nor space, nor deep, nor high
> Can keep my own away from me.[42]

Spiritualism, the belief that the living can communicate with the dead, enjoyed a sudden surge of late-Victorian popularity. Before the Hodgsons left for America, it was beginning to be talked about in Manchester, in middle-class circles and among the pit workers. Spiritualist gatherings in public places and drawing rooms were transported from America to an increasingly serious British middle-class audience. Burnett was familiar with its claims. Of a séance in Washington in 1878 she wrote that she 'was visited by a friend who died in England four years ago. There was a lot of blatant humbug going on & some very nice queer things.'[43] Within the spiritualist sphere were claims of healing. Victorian spiritualism emphasized the importance of fresh air, exercise, and diet. A healthy body was thought to assist the spirit to immortality.

Owen, in her study of Victorian spiritualism, argues that its emergence coincided with a reappraisal of the female role. Women were considered to be more receptive than men, and since communication with the dead was achieved through a channel of self-abnegation, a successful medium reinforced the female icon, while at the same time she subversively established her power.[44] Likewise Ysabel has a dual role: she is rich, denoting power, but unworldly, denoting vulnerability. Despite youth and innocence, her other-world knowledge gives her power. Through a parallel process of authorship, Burnett created her own power. The wealth from her books gave her unfeminine authority, which she continued to wield indirectly, since her characters voice her thoughts through the medium of her pen – another example of Victorian female power hidden behind a curtain of female convention. In a similarly veiled disguise Burnett hid her iron determination beneath a surface of frivolity, in the soft floating clothes she liked to wear and the nickname she encouraged – Fluffina.

Burnett never followed any outward show of Christianity. Private Bible study was another matter, and she copied out her favourite passage many times: 'Whatsoever things are true, whatsoever things are honest, whatsoever things are lovely, whatsoever things are of good report, if there be any virtue, think on these things.'[45] She was not a spiritualist, though she adhered to some of its tenets. Principally she believed in will to propel the self through vicissitudes to triumph. She frequently put her thought into her books. 'I believe black thoughts breed black ills to those who think them I believe the worst – the very worst cannot be done to those who think steadily – steadily only of the best,' says Betty in *The Shuttle*.[46] In *The Dawn of a Tomorrow*, Glad, the cockney heroine who inspires prostitutes, thieves and a would-be suicide, declares: 'What I ses is – if things ain't cheerfle, people's got to be.' Glad, like Burnett, is a would-be fairy godmother: 'If I 'ad a wand...if I 'ad money',[47] but without either she brings joy to the down-and-outs by making them think positively. 'If you fill your mind with a beautiful thought there will be no room in it for an ugly one,' says the king in a fairy story, *Land of the Blue Flower*.[48] 'Two things cannot be in one place. "Where you plant a rose, my lad, a thistle cannot grow",' says the authorial voice in *The Secret Garden*.[49]

When Burnett's landlord sold Maytham Hall in 1907, Burnett finally left England for America. She began building a new house and garden in 1908 on some land she had bought in Long Island. Here *The Secret Garden* was written in 1911. She never stopped writing or having an open mind. She was entranced by the possibilities of cinema, when films were made out of her books. Eight more books followed *The Secret Garden* until her death in 1924, aged nearly 75. Old age crept up on her painfully, though Vivian, who could always be relied on to give meaning and reassurance to life, gave her great pleasure with his marriage in 1914, which brought Burnett two granddaughters.

In 1917 Burnett was sued for libel after describing her nephew's wife to her nephew's wife's sister as 'a liar, slanderer, ill-bred meddler, a shrew, and a brawler of doubtful ante-cedents, and subject to brainstorms'. She wrongly assumed family loyalty would forgive her insults. The episode highlights Burnett's poor judgement of people she knew well. Since the letter was a private communication, the case was dismissed, but it nevertheless shattered her. The press flung poisoned darts. 'She inhabits a saccharine world of her own.' 'She is insufferably rude.' 'She crowns her venerable head with the coiffure of a Titian of twenty.'[50] Burnett never quite enjoyed the closure of happiness she gave her characters.

She remained convinced, nevertheless, that her resolute idealism revealed a greater truth than everyday banality. She liked an anecdote in which Watts was reprimanded for his unrealistically beautiful painting of Covent Garden Market. 'I have never seen it look like this,' said his critic. Watts replied, 'Don't you wish you could?'[51] A short story in 1894, 'Piccino',[52] shows exactly how she turned a real event into a paradigm. Piccino is a little Italian peasant boy, bought by an eccentric, rich, aristocratic English lady because of his incredible beauty. Appalled at his new regime of soap, fine clothes and nursery food, Piccino lasts two days before he runs back to happiness and his dirty familiar life. In the story, Burnett condemns his buyer's selfish whim and upholds the importance of family roots. 'Piccino' was based on fact.[53] In the 1880s in the South of France, Burnett had met a Madame de Noailles – English, rich and eccentric. In 1865 Madame had bought Maria Pasqua, a 7-year-old Italian peasant girl and an artist's model. Madame had first wanted to buy her portrait, but, outbid by a Rothschild, decided to own the original instead. Maria Pasqua was brought up to be an English lady, lost her family, and was unhappy all her life. Burnett's transformation of Maria Pasqua's lifelong misery to Piccino's rapturous freedom shows how she felt happy endings lent power to her convictions. Likewise she based her most enduring stories in realism, spiralling to fairy-tale closures. A study of these – Little Lord Fauntleroy, A Little Princess, and The Secret Garden – shows how in this way Burnett touched universal themes.

INSIDE STORY

In Little Lord Fauntleroy, Cedric Errol is brought from poverty and anonymity in New York and parted from his mother to live with his rich, unpleasant grandfather, the Earl of Dorincourt, whose title and estates he will inherit. Beautiful Cedric works miracles through his sunny nature and loving heart; he turns his grandfather into a happier, nicer man who adores his grandson, grows fond of his hated American daughter-in-law, drops his meanness and becomes a beneficent landowner. A plot to supplant Cedric is overturned. Cedric is restored and remains 'always lovable because he was simple and loving. To be so is like being born a king.'

The plot draws on fairy tale, legend and Bible. The fairy tale is established as characters and settings are given caricature exaggeration. Cedric's mother, Dearest, is blameless, self-sacrificing and beautiful, the earl an epitome of irascible nobility, the castle 'one of the most beautiful in all England'.[54] Even the earl's dog, 'a huge tawny mastiff'[55] is as majestic as a lion. Cedric articulates Dorincourt Castle's fairy-tale associations: 'It reminds anyone of a king's palace. I saw a picture of one once in a fairy book.'[56] Cedric, described as looking like a fairy prince, is ousted and returned to his kingdom because he triumphs over the temptations that might have deflected him from the path of righteousness. The earl, for instance, unsuccessfully tries to lure Cedric from his mother with the gift of a splendid horse. Cedric, like Cinderella, is rewarded with riches and restored to his birthright. Cedric is not only a fairy-tale figure; a blessed miracle child, he resembles the boys of the Bible. *Little Lord Fauntleroy* is a 'wonder tale' and an exemplum, making 'a symbolic statement about the testing and the power of virtue'.[57] Cedric's inviolable goodness makes him the inheritor of the virtuous early-Victorian Evangelical-child tradition.

The genesis and spin-offs of *Little Lord Fauntleroy* throw light on the way consciousness feeds on story, creating its own myth. The manner in which later readers have interpreted *Little Lord Fauntleroy* is a far cry from the words of its text. In the book Cedric is not merely a golden boy; he is a tough, feisty American democrat, friend equally of working classes and nobility, who rejects conservative codes of behaviour. *Little Lord Fauntleroy*, however, has come to symbolize a myth of perfect Victorian childhood, a myth that runs parallel to another tale: the transposition of the reality of Vivian Burnett to the fantasy of Cedric Errol. Here was a muddle of fact and fiction that set up stories within stories. Burnett let it be known that Cedric's character was based on Vivian. She also let it be known that her illustrator, Lionel Birch, based his drawings on a photograph of Vivian, complete with long curls, lace and knickerbockers, while she was equally at pains to point out that Vivian was in fact a manly, robust boy who often played in clothes torn to shreds. At the same time 'reluctant small boys were forced by their mothers into black velvet suits with lace collars...In Iowa an eight-year-old burned down his father's barn in protest at being dressed like Little Lord Fauntleroy.'[58] Burnett allowed Little Lord Fauntleroy merchandise to be marketed on publication, an early example of the image going beyond the book. So the process of reality-to-story was also a cycle of contradictory stories told to set up a fiction that took off into an independent iconic orbit. Little Lord Fauntleroy became to subsequent generations the butt of jokes, famous for his adorable looks, long hair, polite behaviour and mincing dress, which developed into a definition – a mocking icon – of gentle, girlish boyhood and angelic childhood. In Noel Streatfeild's *The Circus Is Coming* (1938), for instance, Peter's prissy behaviour earns him the insulting nickname of 'Little Lord Fauntleroy'. Thus has been created a misleading image of Victorian childhood and boyhood, very different from the text of *Little Lord Fauntleroy* and Cedric's character, because that is how it suited subsequent generations to read the Victorians. *Little Lord Fauntleroy* is an example of how posterity has created a myth from a story, on this unsound foundation. The double myth, the rags-to-riches prince in disguise who nearly lost but kept his kingdom, and the golden lost world of angelic childhood in a shockingly class-ridden but deliciously romantic Victorian world, supplies a need in the psyche of its perpetuators.

Burnett's next enduring story, *A Little Princess*, evolved over eighteen years. It first appeared as a novella, *Sara Crewe, or What Happened at Miss Minchin's*, in 1888, then as a play, *A Little Unfairy Princess* in 1902, and finally as *A Little Princess* in 1905. The plot remained the same. Sara, the only child of rich, impulsive Captain Crewe, an Indian army officer, is sent to Miss Minchin's fashionable London boarding school, where she is a privileged pupil. Miss Minchin is an unsympathetic, grasping woman. Captain Crewe dies, having lost his entire fortune after entrusting it to a friend who invested it in diamond mines. Miss Minchin makes Sara, now a pauper, work as a skivvy and sleep in the attic. She befriends Becky the scullery maid, and helps her loyal but stupid friend Ermengarde. Sara is saved from despair by her empathy and intelligence and imagination. Finally her fantasies come true; she returns to her grim attic to find it transformed into luxury, as if by magic. This is the secret work of the man next door, Mr Carmichael, and Ram Dass, his Indian servant, who both wanted to make the forlorn child happy. Mr Carmichael is ill, sick with guilt at having thought he'd lost, then regained, the fortune of his friend Captain

Crewe. He has been searching the globe for Sara Crewe. Sara's identity is finally uncovered. At last she finds again fabulous wealth, a home and love.

In the novella, Sara is abrasive. By 1905 her character has softened into an adored mother–teacher figure. All the versions represent the two most important things in Burnett's life. Three Sara Crewes made three times as much money out of one idea, and in delving more deeply into her plot, Burnett was able to blazon ever more clearly her lifelong, unshakable belief in redemption through imagination and idealism, and the joys of unlimited wealth. Sara's growth from the fierce 1888 girl of the novella to the 1905 tender fairy-like princess also charts Burnett's maturing perception of what her mores demanded of successful females. The first Sara 'had promptly begun to hate Miss Minchin'[59] and is rude. The second, more polite Sara knows 'there's nothing so strong as rage except what makes you hold it in'.[60] The key to female achievement, like the key to Victorian behaviour, was disguise. Sara's rebellion is masked by self-control. Her emotion finds its outlet in a secret world of the imagination, while the authorial exposition of her feelings made her a strongly sympathetic heroine at a time when the Angel was beginning to unlock the doors of the House. Sara's mixture of nurturing maternity, magical weaver of tales, and her self-empowering leap from poverty to public recognition, crowns her heroine's role. She is Burnett's most idealized image of herself.

The literary roots of *A Little Princess* lie in a multiplicity of sources. Following a tradition established by Dickens, George Eliot and Charlotte Brontë, its themes are explored through childhood. Like Jane Eyre, Sara's intense emotion creates a potency that conveys authenticity of feeling through the perception of a child. Sara, orphaned like Jane Eyre, is a marginalized victim who conquers adversity through self-belief. But unlike Jane who found madness hidden in the attic, Sara's attic, equally a place for the outcast, is recast as a place where imagination is the saviour of sanity and self-help triumphs over malignity. Jane Eyre was an angry child who, as an adult, learned to control her rebellion, while critics suggest that the first Mrs Rochester, raving in the garret, is her mirror-image. Sara, unlike both Mrs Rochesters, transforms her anger into imaginative power; she is a fairy-tale and Romantic heroine.

Burnett uses the attic as a magical place of change, like the locked upstairs chamber in fairy tales where straw is spun into gold, while she also restates its Brontëan grimness into a place where Sara's intrinsic goodness is powerful enough to change dark into light.

Like *Little Lord Fauntleroy*, *A Little Princess* allies itself to fairy tale in its intertextual references. ' 'Diamond mines' sounded so like the 'Arabian Nights',' says the authorial voice.[61] Sara tells her schoolfriends the story of 'The Little Mermaid'. Becky 'did not look – poor Becky! like a Sleeping Beauty'.[62] Sara herself resembles Cinderella in her original high birth, her demeaning sojourn in the kitchen imposed by Miss Minchin, the wicked stepmother figure, her taunts from fellow-pupils Lavinia and Jessie – the 'ugly sisters', and her final restoration to a position even better than before. The Victorian Cinderella was a popular figure 'rewarded for the Victorian feminine virtues of self-sacrifice, cheerful obedience and quiet beauty'.[63] But Burnett inserts an anti-fairy-tale and feminist slant into her fairy-tale plot to reinforce her message that the ideal could easily be real. Sara is at pains to point out that she is not beautiful. Her hair is short and dark, unlike Cinderella's traditionally golden tresses.[64] She is not submissive but assertive, thus combining the role of self-sacrificing mother – starving herself as she gives five of her six buns to Anne, the beggar – with that of the New Woman.

A Little Princess can be read as a radical and feminist novel that undermines the gentle Angel-in-the-House icon. Sara trounces authority, successfully defying Miss Minchin. She is also an intellectual, 'starving for new books to gobble',[65] her father fondly says, stimulated by Carlyle's *French Revolution*, a linguist, and an inspired teacher. At a time when women were just beginning to be admitted to universities, Sara's academic prowess and heroine status gave girl readers a reassurance that clever girls need not sacrifice their brains, like Charlotte M. Yonge's Ethel May, but were praiseworthy.

To add fuel to feminist fire, all the men in the book are flawed. Captain Crewe is rash. Lottie's father is flighty. Mr Carmichael tries but fails to find Sara. Mr Carrisford nearly dies of brain fever, 'not man enough to stand my ground when things looked black'.[66] Ram Dass plays a magic but marginalized role, echoing an upper-class attitude of imperial Edwardian Britain, which denied equal status to natives of the empire and servants. By contrast, Sara is brave and chivalrous. Her father says, 'If Sara had been a boy and had lived a few centuries ago, she would have gone about the country with her sword drawn, rescuing and defending everyone in distress.'[67] Sara's characteristics are admired, boyish Edwardian heroics. A Little Princess twists the common perception of femininity by showing how Sara achieves heroine-hood not only with conventional female qualities like story-telling and mothering, but also by hijacking traditionally male attributes while the men in the story pale beside her.

Above all, A Little Princess highlights the need for imagination and story. Story both distances through narrative and forefronts through emotion. By storyfying the events in her life, Sara grows in strength as she simultaneously blocks and faces them. She pretends she is a princess. She pretends she knows about the Large Family next door. She glorifies her attic by pretending it is the Bastille. With psychological accuracy, Burnett shows that controlled fantasy is a healthy escape from desolation, and that visualisation is a lever to making things happen. The magical results of Sara's fantasies – she does achieve princess status, she does get to know the Large Family, her attic is transformed into a bower of luxury – illustrate Burnett's conviction that story improves real life.

The Secret Garden is the best-known of Burnett's books. On publication in 1911 it failed to make much impact, though one contemporary critic's comment that it dealt 'almost wholly with abnormal people'[68] still resonates. 'Mary with her odd private games and cold indifference to her parents' deaths, might be diagnosed as preschizoid...Colin...as a classic hysteric.'[69]

In The Secret Garden, disagreeable, orphaned Mary Lennox is sent to Misselthwaite Manor, a huge, bleak house full of secrets on the Yorkshire moors, the home of her reclusive, absentee uncle, Archibald Craven. There she finds a hidden dead garden, locked up by her uncle on his wife's death, and her fearful, hysterical, bedridden cousin Colin. Critics have noted similarity of setting, secrets and cries in the night to Charlotte Brontë's Jane Eyre. In discovering the mysteries, Mary uncovers her own hidden strengths and grows nicer. Together with Dickon, a moorland cottage boy, she restores the garden to life and Colin to health and his father's arms. The garden symbolizes the themes of the book: renewal and the power of nature, the female role and motherhood, which triumph over the darker forces of death, hatred and despair.

The word 'garden' comes from a root word meaning enclosure and protection. The garden in *The Secret Garden* conjures up ancient associations: the myth of Eden, the Waste Land, the return of Proserpine to her mother Ceres, and summer's defeat over winter. Carpenter looks on *The Secret Garden* as the clearest celebration of Arcadia, the quest for the Edenic myth sought by the writers of the 'golden age' of children's literature. It is in his view a magic country like Alice's Wonderland, Barrie's Neverland, Grahame's River Bank world in *The Wind in the Willows*, and A. A. Milne's Enchanted Place, all fantasy escapes to alternate worlds.[70] Burnett's pastoral escape also rattles with other interpretations.

As one historian of the English imagination notes, 'the walled garden is the model of secrecy and enchantment; the English imagination can only grow in a confined space'.[71] Historically, the garden, enclosed and protected, is associated with femality and fertility, while gardens and gardening are a quintessentially English phenomenon. *The Secret Garden* is steeped in Edwardian countryside Englishness, in landscape, dialect and class-structure. Burnett was writing in America, recreating in words the beloved walled rose garden she had made at Maytham Hall where she had written her books in a summer house. Her emphasis on Englishness is clear from the beginning; Mary, sallow, ugly, discontented, feels displaced in India where she makes sterile gardens from rootless flowers. Gardening in home soil makes her happy and good while her looks bloom 'like a blush rose',[72] the most English of flowers.

The garden and Mary (whose name echoes Jesus's mother Mary, the universal mother) share the role of mother. Just as Mary nurtures and beautifies the garden, so it mothers her, improving her character and looks. Both make Colin better; the garden's example, unfurling strong new life, inspires him to leave his wheelchair while Mary wills him: 'You can do it. You can!' Mary's intervention makes other mothers come into the garden. Colin's dead mother returns, underlining the immortality of mother-love: 'Happen she's been in the garden an' happen it was her set us to work, an' told us to bring him here,' says half-magic Dickon.[73] Dickon's mother, Susan Sowerby wears a long blue cloak in the garden, the traditional garb of the Virgin Mary, as the children sing the Doxology. The garden is a metaphor for *The Secret Garden's* interpretation of motherhood in imparting spiritual love, growth, health and beauty.

The garden's abandonment by its creators (Mrs Craven died; Mr Craven rejected it) is echoed by Mary's orphan status. Orphan texts abound in nineteenth-century literature. The orphan hero/heroine severed from the shackles of family ties, is free to embark on a journey of self-discovery. In particular, female orphans, as Reynolds and Humble point out, were used by nineteenth-century women writers as a metaphor for testing female autonomy.[74] The orphan hero/heroine is also a scapegoat, a vulnerable, second-class citizen whose isolation from the family reinforces the strength of orthodox family bonds.[75] Thus the garden's decay and Mary's disagreeableness – the result of family disintegration, highlights their own fragility and that of the family who failed them. But Burnett also uses Mary and the garden as a metaphor of renewal and optimism. Mary improves; the garden was always secretly alive; Mr Craven returns to the garden and his son. Not only is the orphan restored to the family fold, but the orphan facilitates restoration. *The Secret Garden* reinforces the family, while also showing that the most reliable example of strength lies in another ideology: nature.

Feminist critics have been disappointed in the silencing of Mary at the end of the book, as Colin is forefronted. In the final pages she is not even mentioned. She has been running a race with Colin in the garden; Colin wins, bursting out of the door, expelled from its womb-like secret nurture to new life. Mary's withdrawal concurs with a Ruskin vision of womanhood. Mary, mother-like and self-sacrificing, retreats to launch the child.

It is tempting to see in Colin a reconstruction of Burnett's dead son Lionel. Burnett had engraved a mourning locket with the quatrain, 'Farewell to others/ But never we part/ Heir to my royalty/ Son of my heart',[76] a permanent memorial both to her never-ending grief, and to her belief that the dead stay with the living. Colin's neuroses are reminiscent of Stephen Townsend. 'I never saw a human being with such a self-tormenting, nervous temperament,'[77] Burnett confided. 'If I can help Stephen to live that will be another beautiful thing to have done,' she told a friend shortly after Lionel's death.[78] Colin, the beautiful boy who did not die, and his triumphant cry, 'I shall live forever and ever and ever!'[79] immortalizes Lionel and salvages the best of Stephen. The happiest points of all Burnett's relationships were based on motherly love, which is the pivot of *The Secret Garden*, and posits Colin as the final dominator.

Burnett was uninterested in challenging the class system. The servants in *The Secret Garden* stay in their places. Martha, like her biblical namesake, serves and is outshone by a Mary. Her brother Dickon, who can barely read, 'is in the pastoral tradition, which prefers shepherds and shepherdesses to stay in Arcadia'.[80] *The Secret Garden* celebrates and combines the pastoral with Edwardian Englishness, in which rurality and the ruling class march hand in hand with male adulation and primogeniture. The book's closing words, 'Master Colin!', underline Colin-the-heir, while the opening words, 'When Mary...', emphasize Mary-the-mother, who originates events.

If Mary is the Victorian self-abnegatory mother, the Angel not of the House perhaps, but of the garden, she is also a Romantic heroine searching for self. *The Secret Garden* contains contradictory strands. The garden itself has a double secret. It is the Victorian, cloistered, guardian female. But the Victorians were past masters at drawing a curtain over matters understood but deliberately left unsaid. Equally, it stands for sex and fertility. The secret garden bursts with fruitfulness. The robin 'showin' off an' flirtin' his tail feathers'[81] finds a 'bold young madam'[82] who lays 'the Eggs'. Plants reproduce extravagantly. 'Buds – tiny at first but swelling...until they burst and uncurled into cups of scent delicately spilling themselves over their brims.'[83] The garden is a place of rampant sensuality and physical exertion. Mary's first attempt at gardening makes her so hot 'that first she threw her coat off, and then her hat'.[84] Rushing round the garden to find live roses, she 'quite panted with eagerness and Dickon was as eager as she was',[85] and fervently kisses the crocuses. The garden and the act of gardening are a form of passion, in which physicality and beauty arouse the senses. The secret garden is a code for Victorian and Edwardian femininity in which female sexuality was concealed. The fiction of the 'good' Victorian women implied sexually passivity, while her true nature hid behind the fiction. Similarly, the garden is a secret concealing fecundity. Its walls enclose, protect and perpetuate the image of covert female sexual response.

A modern scholar[86] has pointed out the similarities between D. H. Lawrence's *Lady Chatterley's Lover* and *The Secret Garden*. In both books nature is as strong as it is erotic. Dickon, earthy and lower-class, who knows all the secrets of nature, is like Mellors; Colin, crippled, cerebral, masterful and upper-class, is like Sir Clifford Chatterley, while the heroine through Dickon/Mellors becomes healthy and fulfilled. Lawrence mentions Frances Hodgson Burnett in his correspondence; he would almost certainly have known of *The Secret Garden*, but whether or not he deliberately drew on it remains a moot point. *The Secret Garden* continues to challenge and stimulate analysis. Its themes extend beyond its boundaries of period and genre to make it an enduring book.

5

Edith Nesbit

I believe I was moderately good.

(*Long Ago When I Was Young*, 1966)

Nesbit was the author of much forgotten hack work, which included adult novels and horror stories; poetry, in which her real love lay; and children's books that propelled her to renown and remain classics in the canon. She married Hubert Bland, a journalist and writer and ran a household full of children, memorable impromptu parties, famous names and stimulating talk. Nesbit was a dramatic woman with a blazing personality, who erupts like a volcano into children's literature, heralding new ways of looking at children. Nothing about her was without controversy, however, including these verdicts. One modern critic sees her subversion as mere middle-class Victorianism in disguise,[1] while her daughter Rosamund's husband said Bland outshone Nesbit in every way. Some bias may have influenced this view; Rosamund discovered she was not actually Nesbit's child at all, but the daughter of Bland and Nesbit's best friend, who lived with them. Nesbit herself was described by Bernard Shaw as audaciously unconventional. The Blands' Bohemian openness, far removed from the shibboleths of their time, nevertheless concealed a surface homage to nineteenth-century respectability and ricochets of resentment.

As Nesbit lay dying, Iris, her own daughter, asked her if, knowing the highs and lows of her life, she would live it all again. Nesbit said yes, because it had all been so interesting. Iris's question points to a conscious gap between Nesbit's experience and fulfilment. Nesbit's response of interest, not happiness, contrasts with most of her children's books which conclude with finding the heart's desire. Elysium, she suggests is the closure prerogative of fiction, not reality. Her stories, pre-closure, however, are an ironic comment on contemporary mores articulated in her narrative technique of a child's voice, which blurs the adult/child divide. This echoed Nesbit's own old/young nature. She saw herself and some saw her as child-like, though since she was known as 'Madam' or 'Duchess', and had a succession of younger lovers, she was also a priestess among her acolytes. Nesbit's overlapping boundaries overlook prevailing authoritarian standards to anticipate a later social levelling of hierarchical power structures in which adult control and child status are equally significant.

SEEKING THE TREASURE SEEKER

Any would-be biographer of Nesbit has a hard task finding her. She wrote a dozen autobiographical childhood articles for the *Girl's Own Paper* (1896–7) that dwelt deeply on early terrors, but their accuracy was questioned by Nesbit's daughter Iris, who had always understood her mother to have been an exception-ally fearless child. After her death her private correspondence was burned by a wary daughter-in-law. Her friends left contradictory vignettes. Her family split into two camps, natural children and adopted children, and contributed different versions of their parents' marriage. Clearly, few agreed or felt neutral about Nesbit. She whipped up a vortex of emotions around her, like a magician not always in control of his magic wand.

Nesbit was reared in mid-Victorian middle-class respectabil-ity. She was born in Kennington, then a rural outskirt of London. Nesbit forebears were academically inclined. Her father ran a small college, where he taught agriculture and chemistry; her grandfather and uncles were also teachers and scientists. Nesbit's mother, who had another daughter by an earlier marriage, came from Kent, where Nesbit was to spend much of her adult life, and set her stories.

The Kennington home had three acres of land and a farm. There Nesbit, known as Daisy, the youngest of five, spent her first eight halcyon years playing with her two next elder brothers who adored, admired, protected and belittled their sister, just as Oswald and Dicky Bastable treated Alice and Noel, the twins in *The Treasure Seekers* (1899). Nesbit's most recent biographer, Briggs, believes Nesbit's depiction of the twins reflects her dual nature. Noel is a frail poet; Alice is a tomboy. Certainly, like Alice, Daisy enjoyed outdoor energetic exploits, then considered boyish. She was especially proud, as an adult, of being able to bend backwards over a gate. She was a precocious child poet and an admired adult one. Her poems were published alongside those of Oscar Wilde, R.L. Stevenson, Rudyard Kipling and Edmund Gosse.[2] However, she never allows Noel to write good poetry. Instead she sets up a double-edged story; within the text Noel believes in his muse, while text and reader engage in an anti-Noel conspiracy as Nesbit derides his efforts. Nesbit mocks seriousness in Noel's first poem.

> Oh Eloquence and what art thou?
> Ay what art thou? because we cried
> And everybody cried inside
> When they came out their eyes were red –
> And it was your doing Father said.[3]

The Bastable stories first appeared in *The Strand*, an adult magazine, and thus had a crossover adult/child audience. Nesbit's persistence in her crossover stance when Bastable sequels were published as children's books indicates an enjoyment of weaving between child and adult. With one hand she identifies with child thought-process and imagination; with the other she exploits gaps between adult and child under-standing in which she sets up the child, as she does Noel, as both vulnerable and a legitimate target of teasing. Perhaps her maverick stance reflects her own experiences.

Nesbit's father died when she was 4. The halcyon years continued in Kennington as her mother gamely ran the college alone, but petered out with the ill health of her elder sister, Mary, which led her mother to try out warmer climes to cure Mary's consumption. From aged 8 Daisy was sent to boarding schools in England, France and Germany that, she said, 'changed as a place-hunter changes his politics',[4] as Mrs Nesbit pursued health cures for Mary around Europe. Nesbit recalled her peripatetic existence in *Wings and the Child*, her analysis of upbringing and child development permeated with her reminiscences and convictions. 'It is a mistake to suppose that children are naturally fond of change. They love what they know. In strange places they suffer violently from homesickness.'[5]

In her *Girl's Own* autobiographical chapters, posthumously published in *Long Ago When I Was Young*, Nesbit writes tenderly of her vulnerability and littleness. Aged 3 she was frightened of an emu skin kept in a garden shed, until coaxed into stroking it by a kindly pupil of her father's. 'We approached the black feathers, I clinging desperately to his neck, and sobbing convulsively. "No-no-no-not any nearer!" But he was kind and wise and insisted. His big hand smoothed down the feathers.'[6] At one school a teacher scolded her for having rough hair – 'I brushed it for fruitless hours till my little head was sore.' Another 'kept my little body going with illicit cakes and plums and fed my starving little heart with surreptitious kisses and kind words'.[7]

Her self-portrait is of a sensitive, fervent, high-spirited, unhappy child with an uncontrollable imagination. One sister's laughing comment on the cuffs she had painstakingly knitted for her mother, 'They would just fit a coal heaver',[8] pierced her unforgettably. On holiday in France Daisy insisted on seeing the naturally preserved mummies in Bordeaux, thinking they were similar to the embalmed ones in the British Museum 'in dear, dear England'. She made a terrible misjudgement. Skeletons hung by their hair with 'gleaming teeth...empty eye sockets... draped in mouldering shreds of shrouds'.[9] The horror haunted her for life. Meanwhile, she ran away from her various schools quite regularly. At one, a French convent, fervour took a religious turn and she begged her mother, unsuccessfully, for permission to convert to Catholicism. 'I know you will let me. Do write and say so.'[10] Daisy was always coaxing and articulate. (Nesbit finally became a Catholic in her early 40s, following her husband's conversion.) Mrs Nesbit rented country houses, and during her holidays Daisy gloried in endless lush countryside while enjoying wild escapades with her two brothers, exploring, boating, discovering a ghost, and throwing fire-crackers down trombones while the band played on.

High spirits apart, Nesbit's rendition of passionate little Daisy is not like the cheerful, self-confident, 'honour bright' child

heroes and heroines of her children's books. Daisy's introspec-
tive, secretive unhappiness echoes the intense loneliness of
Molesworth's or Burnett's complex characters, which Nesbit
never resurrects in her writing. Despite her fervent autobiographical avowal that 'when I should be grown up I might never
forget what I thought and felt and suffered then',[11] the adult
Nesbit barricaded herself from fictional children who voice, like
Daisy, fierce, individualistic feelings. The straightforward children in her texts seldom have emotional outbursts or develop
their characters. In *The Treasure Seekers*, for instance, Dora is
forever a dull prig, Oswald heroic, Alice as game as a girl can be,
H.O. a cheeky little boy. Nesbit was not interested in
reconstructing or analysing childhood in the context of her
own childhood suffering, even though she claimed she could
understand childhood only through her own past.

> There is only one way of understanding children; they cannot be
> understood by imagination, by observation, not even by love. They
> can only be understood by memory. Only by remembering how you
> felt and thought when you yourself were a child can you arrive at
> any understanding of the thoughts and feelings of children...Even if
> you have now forgotten all that you suffered, the mark of that
> suffering remains on your soul to this day.[12]

The fact that she saw the key to understanding all children,
though she knew each child is unique, through her own
childhood reveals the way her character combined generosity in
wishing to understand with egoism. Unlike Molesworth's
pronouncement on detachment, morals and identification in
writing children's books – 'seeing as [children] see, yet
remaining yourself, never losing sight of what is good for
them'[13] – Nesbit appears to identify totally with her fictional
children, demolishing the barrier between adult narrator and
child reader.

Her fictional children represent her ideal vision of childhood.
Like little Daisy, they are bold, jolly, independent, setting out on
adventures, but unlike Daisy, they have no secret troubles. The
adult Nesbit, embracing the New Woman's emancipation, cut
her hair 'like a boy's...deliciously comfortable',[14] stopped
wearing corsets, smoked, rode bicycles in bloomers, and enjoyed
an unconventional lifestyle. Similarly, she created in her
children's books a new sort of child, whose aim is to be happy

and have fun, released from the anguish of her own experience and the tub-thumping morality of the majority of her literary predecessors. Her final children's book, *Wet Magic*,[15] lines up her battle boundaries between two armies. The child protagonists, helped by angst-free heroes from the books of Mrs Ewing, Marryat and Stevenson, fight and defeat the enemy, the Book Hatefuls, narrowly moralist characters like Mrs Fairchild with her 'admonitory forefinger'[16] and the stern mamma in Maria Edgeworth's *Rosamond* 'who was so hateful about the purple jar'.[17]

When Daisy was 12 Mary was in better health, and the Nesbits returned to England. Mary was engaged to a blind poet, Philip Bourke Marston, a member of the Pre-Raphaelites. For a short time Nesbit was a head-patted child of this cluster of cognoscenti, until consumption killed Mary after all, in 1871. After this tragedy, Mrs Nesbit took a country house, Halstead Hall in Kent, which Nesbit loved. It had a trapdoor to a secret den where she kept her books, opening to the roof where she feasted with her brothers. Its garden, rampant with flowers and fruit, was wild. The adult Nesbit venerated Halstead in nostalgic verse: 'there, all day, my heart goes wandering...', there 'the sacred sweet white flowers of memory grow',[18] and immortalized it in her children's books as she bases her protagonists in rural bliss. It was at Halstead that the teenage Nesbit began to make money selling her verses to well-known, popular journals such as *Good Words* and the *Sunday Magazine*. Halstead gave Nesbit a socially conventional life, exchanging calls and tennis parties with the local gentry, an existence she never repeated and mocked vigorously. In *The New Treasure Seekers* the Bastables find 'ladylike...the beastliest word there is'.[19] In *The Red House* Nesbit scorns 'paying proper little calls and giving proper little dinner parties...the fishmonger [sending] in two proper little whitings with their proper little tales in their mouths'.[20] *The Red House*, an adult novel, resurrects both Halstead and the favourite house of her marriage, Well Hall in Kent. The book celebrates Nesbit's exultation in being unconventional. Len and Chloe, the husband and wife protagonists, inherit a rambling house and grounds. As in her own marriage, they both earn; Len writes, Chloe illustrates. They concoct a picnic for their first meal in the Red House: tinned salmon and cocoa set on newspapers – no tablecloth, no whitings – described as a sublime feast. Nesbit ran her life on a similar jolly resourcefulness.

In 1875 Mrs Nesbit, suddenly in straitened circumstances, left Halstead for a small house in Islington, London, dismissed by Nesbit as 'sordid ugliness'.[21] Little detail emerges from this stage of her life since she took care to shroud it in mystery.

Nesbit met her future husband, Hubert Bland, a brush manufacturer, in 1877 through the bank clerk she was then engaged to. The following year she was engaged to Bland. Bland, handsome, clever, amusing, had a mesmerizing personality. H. G. Wells later described him as 'under an inner compulsion to be a seducer...not so much a Don Juan as a Professor Juan'.[22] Wells, by the time he wrote this, may have had his own critical agenda since Bland had foiled Wells's elopement with his daughter Rosamund. Bland, however, certainly enjoyed illicit affairs. While wooing Nesbit, he conducted a relationship with his mother's paid companion, Maggie Duran, who soon bore him a son. This affair lasted for a decade.

Nesbit, aged 21 and unmarried, became pregnant by Bland. Her warm and enquiring nature led her down paths apparently unbarred by any of the usual Victorian strictures of upbringing. Nesbit's novel *Daphne in Fitzroy Street* (1909), the story of a daring schoolgirl who escapes from her boring, suburban relations, sets up home in Bohemian Bloomsbury among artists, and is loved by two men, shows how Nesbit saw nothing wrong in bold behaviour. Daphne, just out of school, passionately kisses St Hilary, a man whom she'd met only once before. They are on a train together. 'There came a pause. It was a pause that called imperatively for something to fill it. She looked at him; her eyelids dropped deeply. He looked at her, and his look compelled the answer of lids re-raised. Slowly they leaned together...'[23] The Mills and Boon element in this otherwise serious novel shows, unusually for its period, the heroine sexually as eager as the man. Daphne embraces all new experiences, deliberately discarding stuffy middle-class conventions, very much like the young Nesbit.

Nesbit and Bland lived together in lodgings but Bland returned home every week to see his mother and Maggie. Nesbit called herself 'Mrs Bland', and peddled her poetry around Fleet Street to earn her living. They married in a registry office when Nesbit was seven months pregnant with her son Paul. Nesbit was so shaken that she put the wrong Christian name for her father on the marriage certificate. Later that year when filling out the 1881 census form, Bland was staying with his mother, and styled himself unmarried. Nesbit found out about his affair when pregnant with her second child, Iris, and, determined to ignore usual norms, befriended the mistress.

By this time, Bland's business had failed, like Father's in *The Treasure Seekers*. He also contracted smallpox which spoiled his looks but not his libido. Nesbit earned their keep by painting greetings cards and selling her writing. She encouraged Bland to write too, launching him on a brilliantly successful career as a journalist and essayist. They wrote novels together and, now less poor, moved regularly to bigger houses and employed more servants. Despite their bourgeois advancement they were fervent socialists and founder members of the Fabian Society, a group dedicated to the reconstruction of society. Fellow members were as interesting as themselves; they included Sidney Webb, the social reformer, and George Bernard Shaw with whom Nesbit fell deeply in love. Shaw responded with lofty inhibitions. 'It is only natural that a man should establish friendly relationships with the wives of his friends,' he told his biographer, 'but if he is wise he puts all idea of sex out of the question.'[24] Whether or not Shaw always lived up to his wisdom, his affair with Nesbit was certainly riddled with turmoil.

For Nesbit, love and hate for Shaw battled equally. She explores a similar relationship in *Daphne in Fitzroy Street*. Daphne loves an artist, Henry, who asks Daphne to run away with him; Daphne is thrilled, but Henry, more devoted to his art, changes his mind. Daphne struggles to comprehend 'that there were two elements she could not control, her love for Henry and Henry himself'.[25] She 'would hate [him] if she did not so terribly, so desperately, love him',[26] and wants to 'hurt him as he hurt me'.[27] Daphne's feelings for Henry echo Nesbit's feelings for Shaw, which she put into her poem about their affair, 'Bewitched'.

> And all would be nothing to suffer,
> If once at my feet you could lie,
> And offer your soul for my loving –
> Could I know that your world was just I –

And could laugh in your eyes and refuse you,
And love you and hate you and die![28]

Though *Daphne* ends with Daphne in Henry's arms at last, she is disillusioned and disenchanted.

Shaw privately told Nesbit's first biographer, Moore, that she wanted to leave Hubert and run away with him.[29] The authorial voice in *Daphne* pronounces:

> you fall in love with people not because they are handsome or clever or good – oh, certainly never because they are good – but because they are lovable. No, not that either, but – because they are the people you fall in love with.[30]

Nesbit, likewise, was ruled never by expediency but by passion and opportunity. In *Wings and the Child* (1913), her book about upbringing, Nesbit writes with admiration of adults who remain childish at heart, citing as examples, the works of Hans Christian Andersen, R. L. Stevenson and Juliana Ewing. Her analysis, however, reads like self-analysis. Such people

> will never learn prudence, or parsimony, nor know, with the unerring instinct of the really grown-up, the things that are not done by the best people. All their lives they will love, and expect love – and be sad, wondering helplessly when they do not get it...If these children, disguised by grown-up bodies, are ever recognised for what they are, it is when they write for and about children.[31]

Nesbit loved and expected love from Shaw and Bland, but, like Daphne, struggled to understand that she might not get it. Experience showed her that to be Bland's wife meant sharing him. Her children's book *The Magic City* (1910) begins with the unhappiness of Philip, the child hero, in sharing his adored grown-up sister, Helen, with the man who loves her. Finally, like Nesbit, he adapts, after trials in a magic world racked by his jealousy. Not till 1917, in her second marriage, aged 59, 'happier now than I ever was', as she told a friend, did Nesbit 'know what it is to have a man's whole heart'.[32]

Meanwhile, her mixture of impulsive generosity and naïvety plunged her into difficulties. Her third child, Fabian, was born in 1885, and six months later she was pregnant again. Her friend Alice Hoatson, a journalist and fellow-Fabian, came to stay to nurse her through the birth, and fell under Bland's spell.

Nesbit's baby died. Her grief was violent, and she refused to part with the baby for burial. 'For one hour and a half I struggled to get it from her,' said Alice,[33] who had prepared a long fish basket with flowers, while Bland dug the grave in the garden. Alice by this time was pregnant herself by Bland. Nesbit did not know who the father was, though Alice may have thought she did. Unmarried, Alice was now unmarriageable and disgraced. Nesbit solved her predicament by offering to adopt the baby and let Alice stay permanently as companion-house-keeper. According to Alice's daughter Rosamund, Nesbit had encouraged Bland to interest himself in Alice, to deflect him from a woman she disliked. 'It was my own fault. I might have prevented the opportunity. I didn't and I deserved the consequences,' Nesbit commented later.[34]

Alice was the calm arbiter of household and children, while the volatile Nesbit alternately blazed with rages or blossomed with urbanity. All the children called Alice 'auntie'. The Blands called quiet Alice 'Mouse'; they called each other 'Cat'. Nesbit's attitude to a mouse-like character is crystallized in Daisy Foulkes, nicknamed the White Mouse, in *The Wouldbegoods* and *The New Treasure Seekers*. Irritating and timid – she faints when she is frightened – the hearty Bastables despise her. Finally, the Oswald/Nesbit narrator concedes, unenthusiastically, 'she was not a bad sort of kid', though never 'free and happy'.[35] Daisy, like Alice, teeters on the brink of Nesbit's sufferance. Interestingly, Nesbit gave Daisy her childhood nickname, both recalling and distancing herself from her vulnerable child self. The Bastables at first thought Daisy Foulkes's father was a robber, though he was actually their own father's friend. Daisy, daughter of 'Our Robber' who was not really a robber, underlines Nesbit's ambivalent attitude to Alice, the thief of Bland's affections, but not a real thief as she could not, as Nesbit could, claim her children, or the name of Mrs Bland.

Nesbit frequently centres her children's fiction on the failure of a supposedly good idea, just as her own naïve good intentions towards Alice resoundingly backfired on her. Her child protagonists are regularly baffled by the disastrous results of their incursions in an adult world. In *Five Children and It*, Cyril, Robert, Anthea and Jane are granted wishes that turn sour as child naïvety meets adult superiority. In *The Wouldbegoods*, the

Bastables' 'society for being good in' inspires them to high aspiration and drops them in dire consequences: for instance they weed a poor widow's garden, then discover they have denuded it of all her vegetables planted by her soldier son, missing, believed dead. Nesbit is partly mocking early nineteenth-century moralist children's literature, specifically naming *Ministering Children*, in which children perform good deeds to lead them to eternal life. At the same time, disillusion was etched into her consciousness. Disenchantment haunts her childhood memoirs. Once she was appalled by a visit to a French shepherdess who was not, as she imagined, a Watteau beribboned maiden, but a hideous old hag. She suffered agonies when her mother fetched her from school not on the day she hoped, but a few days later. Her experiences, like the crypt in Bordeaux when the mummies turned out to be, not as she expected, safely wrapped in bandages but beckoning skeletons, are evoked with the nightmare intensity of shattered dreams.

In her children's texts, the disillusioned heroes and heroines are saved from their predicaments either by magic or by an unlikely happy ending that turns her non-magic books into fairy tales. 'I can't help it if it is like Dickens. Real life is often something like books,'[36] says Oswald at the happy conclusion of *The Treasure Seekers*. Nesbit's example of fiction to prove the realistic nature of her own fiction is a double bluff that reinforces the unlikeliness of her proposal that real life ends up happily ever after. The horror of Nesbit's child protagonists when they magically grow up, and their disappointment in their granted wishes, shows that Nesbit found childish hopes to be illusory but more pleasant than adulthood with its broken illusions. Whether Nesbit saw herself as swindled by her naïvety, or whether she wished to warn her readers that good intentions implode, her children's books show a mischievous world in wait upon the gullible. 'Life is often very unfair and enough to stop anyone trying to do a noble action,'[37] she declared in *Five of Us, and Madeline*. Ironically, this posthumous publication was edited by Rosamund, Nesbit's constant proof of her own naïvety.

The Blands' open marriage, H. G. Wells noted, 'E. Nesbit not only detested and mitigated and tolerated but presided over and I think found exceedingly interesting'.[38] Such disparate verbs indicates Nesbit's mercurial nature. Everyone enjoyed knowing the Blands. Their stimulating hospitality was legion. Well Hall, at Eltham in Kent, to which they moved in 1899, was Nesbit's favourite house, with its moat, ghost, rambling rooms and garden. There Nesbit lived for over twenty years, and wrote her best children's books. The novelist Berta Ruck described its atmosphere: 'open house, riotous, populous, extravagant. The difficulty at Well Hall was to know when it was a party and when it was the usual 'House Full'.[39]

But the atmosphere was also explosive. Rosamund remembered mealtimes interrupted as Nesbit stormed off in a temper, to be coaxed back by Bland. Nesbit enjoyed drama: 'that's what keeps women alive'.[40] She created her own; after Shaw she began to have affairs with younger men. To one of them, the poet, Richard le Gallienne, Nesbit 'suggested adventure, playing truant, robbing orchards and such boyish-like pranks'.[41] She could also be didactic and intolerant. Ruck noted

> When she said of people encountered, 'Dear, I didn't like them!' it was Finis. She was a Socialist of pioneer views. Yet I have heard her complain of some illustration that made her characters 'look as if they weren't the children of gentlefolk'.[42]

Contradictions abounded: childish, sensual; boyish, romantic; kindly, volatile; generous and prejudiced.

The Well Hall years began with tragedy. Nesbit, now 40, suffered a stillbirth, while Alice, still indispensable to Bland, gave birth to John, whom Nesbit adopted and loved, though Alice was the one who looked after him. In 1900, Nesbit's own son, Fabian, aged 15, died after an operation to remove his adenoids. This was a common operation, carried out at home, but Fabian, intelligent, rebellious, of all the Bland children the most like Nesbit, failed to come round from the anaesthetic. Rosamund, aged 13, heard Nesbit shout at Bland, 'Why couldn't it have been Rosamund?',[43] confirming her hunch that her mother did not like her. Nesbit was tortured by her memories of punishing Fabian for naughtiness; once he had lied about taking some sweets intended for poor children. 'Do you understand, remember, forgive? It is your mother who has them to remember.'[44] Rosamund and John learned the truth about their parentage later, but to many of the Blands' friends it was common knowledge and proof of their unconventional, convivial ménage. For none of the Blands can it have been so easy. Throughout her marriage, Nesbit wrote constantly to pay the bills. Novels and poetry poured from her pen. She dubbed her novels pot-boilers and saw herself as a poet. Though the poet Henley urged her not to 'run the risk of breathlessly making too many',[45] her poetry was highly regarded, as was her opinion. In 1895 she was asked, with other poets, to suggest a successor to the poet laureate Tennyson.[46] However, she did not find her unique voice until *The Treasure Seekers* appeared in 1899. Her inspiration was Oswald Barron, a journalist and historian, ten years younger than Nesbit, and her lover. Both were dynamic; both knew Blackheath well, the Bastables' setting. Barron encouraged Nesbit to rekindle her childhood, and fired her sense of history. As Briggs points out, Nesbit began writing *The Treasure Seekers* after the death of her adored elder brother. Another brother was in Australia; her sister Mary had died many years before. Nesbit had always liked taking those she loved to see her childhood homes. Now she recreated her happy long-ago atmosphere, resuscitating for Barron a childhood 'identical but for the accidents of time and space' as she spelt out her dedication to him.

The genesis of *The Treasure Seekers* and its authorial child-and-adult voice illuminates the way Nesbit's mind worked. The book celebrated Nesbit's affair with Barron; it also recalled her childhood. To Nesbit, love and remembering were potent deities. Shortly after publication, Nesbit lost Barron to his own happy marriage. He exemplifies Nesbit's vision of the transience of childhood happiness, as well as her experience of the unreliability of adults. Though subtext points to adult ineptness (Father is useless at making money) and child insecurity (poverty and a dead mother), the children form a united band of jollity and optimism, a separate unit from the adults. What Nesbit liked best was adults who were for ever children. As she explained in *Wings and the Child*, 'Deep in [the grown-up's] heart is the faith and hope that in the life to come it may not be necessary to pretend to be grown-up.'[47] Nesbit echoes Wordsworth's *Intimations of Mortality*: 'birth is but a sleep and a forgetting'. Her vision of childhood is a Romantic distillation of separation, integrity and eternity that accorded with an Edwardian escapist dream of youth, nostalgia and fun.

The seam, once opened, rapidly yielded more treasure. Two volumes of magical short stories followed: *The Book of Dragons* (1899) and *Nine Unlikely Tales for Children* (1901) The Bastable sequels, *The Wouldbegoods* and the *New Treasure Seekers* were published in 1901 and 1904. *Five Children and It* and its sequel *The Phoenix and the Carpet* followed in 1902 and 1904. *The Story of the Amulet* and *The Railway Children* appeared in 1906, *The Enchanted Castle* in 1907, *The House of Arden* in 1908, *Harding's Luck* in 1909, *The Magic City* in 1910, *The Wonderful Garden* in 1911, *The Magic World* in 1912 and *Wet Magic* in 1913. She was equally industrious on other levels; in 1909, for instance, as well as *Harding's Luck*, she wrote a book of short stories, a play – *Cinderella* – two long adult novels and a volume of verse.

Plenty of money was coming in, and none was saved. When Bland died unexpectedly in 1914, Nesbit, whose creative powers had by this time dried up, was suddenly at a loss for income. She decided to run Well Hall commercially, taking in paying guests, and selling its garden produce. A Fabian supporter, a friend of Bland's, saw how Nesbit shivered, peddling her vegetables in the garden, and put up a hut for her with a gas heater. This was Thomas Tucker, a marine engineer, known to all as 'the Skipper', 'the best man I have ever known',[48] Nesbit called him. The Skipper admired and adored her, and in 1917, three years after Bland's death, they married. The Skipper was 60, Nesbit a year younger. Many of Nesbit's family and friends were surprised since 'he never wore a collar and hadn't an aitch in his head'.[49] Paul and Iris were dismayed; only Rosamund liked him and supported her. Nesbit was back on a favourite, familiar podium, the revered priestess receiving homage from the humble, as well as a completely novel pedestal of devoted monogamy. Her marriage, she said, gave her 'the happiest years of my life'.[50]

Well Hall, still too expensive to run, was sold, to Nesbit's sorrow. The Tuckers converted two huts near Dymchurch, Kent, used by the Air Force during the war, renaming them the 'Long Boat' and the 'Jolly Boat'; the connecting passageway was the 'quarterdeck gangway.' Her capacity for friendship continued. The playwright and songwriter Noel Coward, then aged 21, was an enthralled visitor and a lifelong admirer. When he died aged 74 in 1973, he had *The Enchanted Castle* on his bedside table. Age and illness crept up suddenly on Nesbit. 'I don't make the money, or have the parties, or see the people I did. I'm ill. I'm often in pain, but – I'm happier now than I ever was,' she told a friend.[51] A lifelong smoker, she developed bronchial problems and died in 1924, aged 66.

She wanted no memorial stone on her grave, but the Skipper carved her name in wood, followed by the words 'poet and author'. Shortly before she died she told a friend

> When we were at Well Hall I used often on summer evenings to slip away from the table and look through the window at the rest of you among the fruit and flowers and bright glasses, and think, 'This is how I shall see it all some day when I am not alive any more.'[52]

Nesbit was a nonconformist, an outsider, an observer, an ardent player. In her will, she left her property to be divided among the Skipper, Paul and Iris. There was nothing for Rosamund and John. Rosamund, she felt, had enough, while Bland had left his small estate not to Nesbit but to John, though it was so inadequate that Shaw helped pay his Cambridge fees. A similar legacy of hurt echoed through all the relationships of Nesbit's life, except for her second marriage. She never lost her zest for living, however. Dying, she wrote, 'The human span of life is far too short. What things there are still to see and to do and to be and to grow into and to grow out of!'[53] Her curiosity and fervency, which she proudly claimed were child-like, were unquenchable.

THE ENCHANTED ESCAPE

Coveney suggests that the end of the century saw childhood as 'a regressive escape into the emotional prison of self-limiting nostalgia'. Artists 'indulged nostalgia because they refused or failed to come to sensitive terms with the cultural realities of the time'.[54] Nesbit's exploration of childhood, however, was not so much a regression to an emotional prison as a longing for a visionary idyll. Her children's books are about escape. Her child protagonists are a vehicle of her vision, which celebrates the power of the imagination. Nevertheless her presentation of children shows a complex ambivalence that echoes the conflicts between her own political agendas and conventional Edwardian mores. She shows how restrictive upbringing brings out the worst in adults and children, creating unhappy power struggles. In a magical short story, 'The Cockatoucan',[55] for example, Matilda wriggles and swells herself inside her tight uncomfortable dress until she bursts her hooks and seams. Pridmore, her strict, disagreeable nurse is turned by magic into an Automatic Nagging Machine, eager to spew out upbringing maxims, but disabled, unless fed with coins, which, naturally, Matilda refuses to do.

Nesbit's books denounce strict grown-ups: Aunt Enid in *Wet Magic*, who 'was what is called 'firm' with children';[56] Aunt Emma in *The Railway Children*, who 'believed in keeping children in their proper places';[57] Aunt Maud in *Harding's Luck*, who sneers at imaginative Dickie, the boy hero – all impose unreasonable rules. The child protagonists escape from their aunts (a private dig at Alice?) to find fulfilment in a magic or child-orientated world. The 'vinegar aunt', a stock figure in Victorian children's literature (Elizabeth Wetherell's *The Wide, Wide World*, Frances Hodgson Burnett's *Two Little Pilgrims' Progress*, Charlotte M. Yonge's *Countess Kate*) frequently capitulated to the charms of her charges, while Nesbit uses her as a symbol of adult repression from which children must break free to explore their individuality and independence.

Nesbit only writes approvingly of adults who level themselves with children. In *The Railway Children* Bobbie comments after Mother's outburst, 'Isn't Mother splendid? You catch any other grown-up saying they were sorry they had been angry.'[58] Mrs Leslie, the lady poet in *The Treasure Seekers*, is 'like a jolly sort of grown-up boy in a dress and hat'.[59] Kathleen in *The Enchanted Castle* remarks, 'if you want grown ups to be nice to you, the least you can do is be nice to them',[60] equalizing the adult/child relationship.

While Nesbit the woman delighted in finding herself child-like, Nesbit the narrator has an air of superiority over the child reader and the child in the book. Though Nesbit appears to be on the side of the child, her interpretation of 'child' is a moveable concept. Although in her view the only worthwhile adults are those who express the child within, she presents childhood as a state of folly curable by the wisdom that comes with adulthood. Her fictional children frequently lack judgement. For instance, *Five Children and It* is the tale of Robert, Anthea, Cyril and Jane and a sand-fairy, the crotchety Psammead, the touchstone of the story. It has a dual role, representing both their fantasy and parental dictates as it grants their wishes while frequently pointing out their want of 'good tempers, or common-sense, or manners'. 'You have no more sense than so many oysters.'[61] 'They're sure to wish for something silly.'[62] The children become beautiful, rich, and able to fly; their sweet but irritating baby brother becomes universally wanted (a careless wish to get rid of him) and grows up; their house becomes first a castle, then stalked by Red Indians. Each wish not only turns out badly but denies the children food, or makes sustenance hard to find. When they are beautiful, Martha, the maid, refuses to feed them because they are unrecognizable; their gold coins are illegal tender and they cannot buy any food; flying makes them hungry, but since people are too terrified of them to give them anything, they swallow their morals instead and steal from a clergyman's larder window; their dinner during the besieged castle episode is invisible and unfeelable, only materializing when bitten, so that the meal is a messy affair. The subtext warns that the exercise of imagination is insubstantial, risky or uncivilizing. The text confirms the very authoritarian view that children are silly, too inexperienced to know what is best for them.

The children's naïvety and need of adult supervision is hammered home by the failure of their wishes. Ultimately, the book polarizes children and adults, so that 'adult authority becomes reinscribed in the text as the source of knowledge'.[63] On one level the book celebrates child playfulness and autonomy. The four children roam on holiday without their parents; Martha, the maid, is bewitched into not noticing their wishes. Although *Five Children and It* looks like a carnivalesque text, the normative world remains unchallenged as Nesbit uses playfulness as a mirror of child gullibility and foolishness. The children are set up both as a pillory of foibles as well as a fount of originality and imagination. The status of the child in the mind of the reader varies. The narrator's voice gives separate storylines to the adult and child reader. 'Grown-up people find it very difficult to believe really wonderful things, unless they have what they call proof. But children will believe almost anything, and grown-ups know this,'[64] Nesbit explains in the first chapter. Thus she grounds her fantasy in a tease on child trustfulness, just as she teases her child protagonists and readers, presenting them with a veneer of emancipation that barely conceals their folly.

The Victorians and Edwardians enjoyed a black humour that highlighted and protected them from the harsh vicissitudes of daily life. Sam Weller in *Pickwick*, for instance, told a story of a 'clever pieman' who seasoned kittens 'for beefsteak, weal, or kidney, 'cording to the demand'.[65] Harry Graham's popular *Ruthless Rhymes for Heartless Homes* (1899) employed the same barbarity for children: 'Billy in one of his nice new sashes/ fell in the fire and was burnt to ashes./ Now although the room grows chilly/ I haven't the heart to poke poor Billy.'[66] At the same time there was an enjoyment of 'high jinks'. Queen Alexandra and her son 'would recall with sentimental pleasure the way in which they had squirted each other with soda-water siphons during the Christmas festivities at Sandringham'.[67] Edwardian families allowed their children more latitude than the previous generation. Nesbit's child characters were typical of the way contemporary upper- and middle-class children were allowed to play roughly and adventurously. At the same time her apparently opposing attitudes to her child characters, her appreciation and mockery of child naïvety, was of its period. Children, who had a generation earlier been venerated as angelic heralds, were fair game for ridicule in the late-Victorian climate of topsy-turveydom.

Her method is made clear in *The Red House* (1902) and *The New Treasure Seekers* (1904), in which the same event is written from an adult and child viewpoint respectively. The Bastables pretend to be antiquaries and bamboozle their way to reading would-be learned papers at the Red House, home to the just-married Len and Chloe. In *The Red House* a furious Chloe, about to throw the trespassers out, is disarmed by their good manners (the boys doff their caps), good clothes (the girls wear many-caped coats) and good looks. They

> talked to us with simple directness: of adventures, of literature, of the ways of providence, and their vital ambitions. What struck me most was their confident assumption that now we knew them we could not help liking them...Oswald evidently thought a great deal

of himself, but, as I could not but reluctantly acknowledge, with some justice! They were extremely 'free in their talk' but never vulgar. They were very much funnier than they meant to be.[68]

Chloe, by now enchanted, insists on giving them lunch. The doting Len notes approvingly, 'Chloe had become one of the children, and was the most childlike of all.' The children 'have electrified, bewildered, enlightened. They are very trusting. The world must have been kind to them.'[69]

Here are hallowed totems of Edwardian middle-class childhood: no vulgarity, frankness, self-confidence, melting charm and appearance. Nesbit sets up the icon, both to approve it and to crush it. The Bastables captivate, but, 'much funnier than they meant to be', they satirize child sentimentality to an adult audience. Meanwhile, in facilitating the regression of Chloe, they reiterate Nesbit's favourite theme, that while children are a legitimate butt, the best adults are childish.

Rewritten in *The New Treasure Seekers*, the story is the same, with Nesbit's satire more subtly concealed. This chapter first appeared in the *London Magazine* in 1904; like the other Bastable stories, it was written for a crossover audience, aimed at the entire family. Children understood in that family literature, as in family life, there were certain things beyond their understanding, which explains Nesbit's levels of meaning in her children's books and varying relationship with her text and her readers. She contrasts the naïvity of her child characters with the sophistication of her readers, as in *The Wouldbegoods*.

> if you are very grown-up, or very clever, I daresay you will now have thought of a great many things. If you have you need not say anything, especially if you're reading this aloud to anybody. It's no good putting in what you think in this part because none of us thought anything of the kind at the time.[70]

Her double messages are present throughout the Bastable books. In *The New Treasure Seekers*, for instance, the Bastables can't decide whether to ask permission to be antiquaries, 'so we tossed for it, only Dora had feelings about tossing up on a Sunday, so we did it with a hymn-book instead of a penny'.[71] Mockery of Victorian Sunday piety and child ingenuousness vie equally with a cheerful approval of play.

The Victorians and Edwardians revered rank, whether of class, work or family. Nesbit's portrait of Oswald as a figure of satire reinforces adult power in a hierarchical world in which children, subject to authority, languished at the bottom of family ranking. Adults see that Oswald's constant vaunting of superiority is proof of his childishness. 'Oswald knows [Chloe] would have liked his paper best because it was the best, though I say it.'[72] The child reader sees easily that despite his boastfulness Oswald makes disastrous misjudgements, as in *The Wouldbegoods* when Oswald floods the house by leaving his cricket ball in the gutter. Nesbit's satire both questions and ridicules hierarchy and male superiority.

Like society around her, Nesbit revered the familial icon. Although she had unconventional views on fidelity within marriage, she felt the need in her own life to present to the world a united family front. Her fictional children are the offspring of united families; though brothers and sisters squabble like puppies they are fiercely loyal to the family. Family honour is the Bastable watchword. Within her fictional families Nesbit's attitude to gender both reflects and innovates norms. Edwardian girlhood was at a crossroads, with one direction rooted in economic and intellectual dependency, the other aiming for emancipation. Edwardian upper- and middle-class families were conventionally financed by fathers, while domesticity and femininity were as one. Nesbit's own childhood confuted tradition; she had no father after the age of 3, and her mother organized a peripatetic lifestyle. In working-class families, women as well as men were wage-earners. The Blands' double income echoed the working-class economic power structure, a stance that reinforced their Fabian beliefs in constructing a more equal society.

Her child heroines, like Nesbit herself, combine a typically Edwardian feminine approach to the family with a feisty tomboyishness. Nesbit with her shingled hair, smoking, bicycling and bloomers, enjoyed the epithet of boyish. Her readiness to take lovers was a contradiction of contemporary feminine concepts of reticence and delicacy. Favourite fictional women are similarly boyish and sensual. The lady poet in *The Treasure Seekers*, for instance, is 'like a jolly sort of grown-up boy in a dress and hat'.[73] Daphne's sexual allure in *Daphne of Fitzroy*

Street is presented as a legitimate part of her charm. Nesbit loathes physical frailty, the Victorian hallmark of a ladylike mien. 'Dora, butter fingered as ever, missed the catch.'[74] 'It turned out Daisy was not really dead at all. It was only fainting – so like a girl.'[75] This comment mocks iconic femininity and since it is made by Oswald, a satire of 'the complacent Victorian patriarch in embryo',[76] it shoots a double arrow in simultaneously mocking male superiority.

At the same time, Nesbit's texts constantly and conventionally nominate family harmony as a female domain, echoing Victorian mythic feminine idylls. '[Anthea] remembered what Mother had said about [Anthea] being the eldest girl and about trying to make the others happy.'[77] 'Oh *don't*! It's bad enough to quarrel when you don't want to, but to *set out* to quarrel! Don't,' says Elfrida to her brother in *The House of Arden*.[78] 'When Mother died she said 'Dora, take care of the others, and teach them to be good and make them happy,''[79] Dora blurts to Oswald. 'Oh, *don't*,' Bobbie cries to her Railway Children siblings, 'don't let's be horrid to each other. I'm sure some dire calamity is happening. Don't let's make it worse!'[80]

The Victorian 'angel in the house' was compounded of self-sacrifice and powerlessness set in economic dependency. The Edwardian ideal, as the New Woman demanded recognition, was based upon shifting ideologies. Its variable nature is Nesbit's constant refrain. Her ideal female, much like her own nature, is an expression of emotion and audacious courage. Daring Alice Bastable, 'as near a brick as a girl can go',[81] can undo the most hardened and irate opponent with her charm. 'Everyone is always wanting to kiss Alice.' Nesbit pinpoints Alice's allure in her innovative Edwardian mixture of boyish heroics and female winsomeness.

Nesbit explores overlapping gender roles within family structure more deeply in *The Railway Children*. Here Nesbit questions gender boundaries with Father, Mother, and their children, Roberta, Peter and Phyllis, though the girls are known as Bobbie and Phil. ('What rum names. All boys.')[82] Their life is an Edwardian suburban home idyll that shatters, as the book begins, symbolized by the explosion of Peter's new toy engine. Father proposes to mend it, with everyone's help.

'*Can* girls help to mend engines?' Peter asked doubtfully.
'Of course they can. Girls are just as clever as boys, and don't you forget it.'[83]

In the next paragraph Father is arrested and wrongfully imprisoned. The engine remains broken; the capable provider fails to live up to his role of middle-class *pater familias* invulnerability. Now Mother assumes a joint masculine and feminine role as she organizes a new home and supports her family by selling her writing, one of the few acceptable female forms of earning. However, her earning powers are weak; the family must do without warmth and nice food when she fails to sell her work. Family security is seen as a precarious nirvana and sex equality appears aligned with fragile resources.

Bobbie, aged 12, is leaving the carefree irresponsibility of childhood for the adult role of mother, which she combines with a male-like authority. She transforms the course of events. It is she who gets the toy engine mended, defuses sibling quarrels, organizes the barely affordable doctor's bill, nurses her ill mother, orchestrates the return of the Russian dissident to his family, and sets in motion the process of freeing her father. 'Mothers never have favourites, but if their Mother *had* had a favourite, it might have been Roberta.'[84] Mother herself, beautiful, home-maker, chief earner and moral arbiter, is given an heroic stance which she bequeaths to Bobbie. Nesbit here sees mothering to be indivisible from ideal womanhood, which itself utterly rejects any lingering 'angel in the house' characteristics, and aspires instead to independence and power.

Nesbit draws a picture of a limited traditional Edwardian male view of womanhood. Bobbie, Phyllis and Peter rescue Jim, a boy who has broken his leg and is stuck in a railway tunnel. Bravely in the dark Bobbie tends Jim, who is first unconscious, then in agony, while the other two get help. Later, at home, Peter finds out that Bobbie feels ill at the thought of blood and teases her about bones crunching to toughen her up. Bobbie then ties Peter up with ropes so tightly that he can't move. The doctor removes Peter to explain matters, man to man.

Men have to do the work of the world and not be afraid of anything – so they have to be hardy and brave. But women have to take care of their babies...and be very patient and gentle...Quite wild beasts [are] immensely gentle with the female beasts Girls are so much softer and weaker than we are...if they weren't, it wouldn't be nice for the babies. Their hearts are soft, too, and things that we shouldn't think anything of hurt them dreadfully.[85]

Bobbie's violent rope-tying reaction has already contradicted a male assumption of female weakness and softness, but both Peter and the doctor have failed to notice. They only appreciate Bobbie's motherly strength in staying with Jim in the tunnel. Peter repeats what he has learned from the doctor. 'Girls are poor, soft, weak, frightened things like rabbits.'[86] However, Peter's manly pretensions to protect his family prove hollow. When they are cold, he is caught dishonourably stealing coal. He boasts emptily of his readiness to fight coal-throwing canal boys, while his sisters tactfully bolster him. 'Throughout the novel, the girls' level of awareness and understanding continually exceeds their brother's, but in a parody of adult feminine strategies they pretend to ignorance in order to feed the male ego.'[87] Nesbit uses gender norms as a tool of analysis, to illustrate society's expectations of male and female, to show the shortfall, and to show how a silent consent to the gap between the two confusingly both continued and undermined the status quo.

The Railway Children highlights the gulf that Nesbit saw between childhood and adulthood. Her children, protected by adults, bask in a kind world. Bad things are kept from them. When Father goes to prison, the children know nothing. Though Bobbie knows something terrible has happened, she consents to the contract of child-ignorance. 'If Mother doesn't want us to know she's been crying, we *won't* know.'[88] When Ruth, the servant, hints at Father's whereabouts, she is instantly dismissed. Mother creates a fool's paradise to maintain child innocence and optimism. When Bobbie inadvertently finds out where Father is, adult knowledge catapults her into an adult conspiracy. Mother asks,

'Are you going to tell the others?'
'No.'
'Why?'
'Because –'
'Exactly. So you understand why I didn't tell you. We two must help each other to be brave.'[89]

The adult–child gulf, Nesbit maintains, is fundamental and instinctive.

As the cruel world impinges, the children are still shielded. They learn the Russian dissident was imprisoned for writing a book of ethics. They are reassured that such gross travesties of justice could only happen in Russia, not England, where people are more fairly punished, says Mother, 'if judges *think* they've done wrong'.[90] Mother still avoids confronting the children with their father's plight. As Nesbit contrasts the charmed world of fatherly railway employees with the fierce, uncouth canal people, she shows that not everyone is well-meaning. The canal people hurl coal to frighten the children off, while their dialect speech affirms their otherness. Nevertheless, Bill the Bargee becomes a friend when the children rescue his baby from his burning barge cabin. Bobbie comments: 'I think everyone in the world is a friend if you can only get them to see you don't want to be *un*-friends.' Mother sighs, 'Perhaps you're right.'[91] Mother will not destroy her children's faith. *The Railway Children* campaigns for a childhood right to innocence and optimism, which adults should reinforce however much their own experience contradicts this ideal. Father's reply, 'Hope? Rather! Tons of it!' to Peter's 'Is there *no* hope?' when his engine explodes, underpins the entire book. Edwardian Bobbie, entrenched in independent New Woman values, driven by love, hope and morality, is as powerful a force for good as her earlier Romantic and Evangelical literary child ancestors.

The Railway Children is also a paean to a Victorian and Edwardian way of thought in which silence was an accepted means of disguise. In the nineteenth- and early twentieth-century world of rule and convention, indiscretions had to be hidden from everyone everywhere for fear of the mythical, eager, judgemental, prying Mrs Grundy. Silence became a discipline in which need and expression were ideally hidden behind a mask of control. Axioms of childhood: 'Hold your tongue'; 'Save your breath to cool your porridge'; 'Children should be seen and not heard'; signals of silence all, spoke of training to a frame of mind in which communication was obfuscated by the ramifications of correct behaviour. Any deviation from the norm was seen as a dangerous loosening of the bolts of middle-class scaffolding. The sanctions were harsh.

Thus the shame of Father's imprisonment means Mother must protect her family by moving from suburbia to rural anonymity. Mother tells her children 'not to ask me any questions, and not to ask anybody else any questions'.[92] When Bobbie discovers 'the terrible secret', Mother tells her they won't mention it again. 'And darling, try not to think of it. It's much easier for me if you can be a little bit happy.'[93] She wants Bobbie to present a front, as she has, far removed from inward feeling. Such pretence, to Victorian and Edwardian eyes, was neither misleading nor hypocritical, but a courageous buttress to the obligations of form.

The Railway Children has proved to be the most enduring of Nesbit's children's books. Its realism is suffused with fairy-tale resonance. The nameless old gentleman who solves all problems, his transport – the train – described by the children as 'a great dragon', is like a fairy godfather. The book's themes of protected childhood and restoration of family idyll are bounded by sentiment and convention. How Nesbit intended The Railway Children to be read and how her contemporary audience received it can only be speculative. The fact of its popularity today suggests a desire for another sort of fairy tale of a nostalgic dream of Edwardiana, optimism and happy endings.

As Katherine Briggs has pointed out, Nesbit's own fairy tales parody the fairy-tale genre. Her fantasy tales, on the other hand, such as Harding's Luck and The Story of the Amulet, are serious critiques of class, politics, and education, achieved by her mixture of magic in a world of realism. Just as Burnett found everyday life enhanced by 'pretending', and wrote as an extension of her thinking, so Nesbit, who needed action and amusement to spice up her existence, felt impelled to show in her children's books how imagination can enrich and endanger. Of all her books, The Enchanted Castle explores the most clearly its ecstasies and horrors, though critics have pointed out its carelessness of construction and language.

Gerald, Cathy and Jimmy, left at school for the holidays in the care of Mademoiselle, the French teacher, play with Mabel, the housekeeper's niece, at a grandiose castle, Yalding Towers. Mabel has found a magic wishing ring that does whatever you say: makes the wearer invisible; nine feet high; grown-up. Mademoiselle nurses a secret sorrow; she is estranged from her lover. He turns out to be Lord Yalding, miserably convinced he'd lost her for ever. The ring facilitates their reunion and finally uncovers heavenly truths. 'Everything is revealed. There are no more secrets. It is a moment and it is eternity. The eternal light rests on and illuminates the eternal heart of things.'[94] The children are blessed with a glimpse of mystical enlightenment.

The corollary of illumination is terror. When Lord Yalding sees Greek statues come alive, he is distraught, convinced he is mad. When the children put on a play and wish for a real audience, the Ugli-Wuglies, the dummy audience that they made out of coat-hangers, hockey sticks, coats and paper masks, come malevolently alive. The children's horror springs from the subconscious fear of the homely made unfamiliar; the connection of the uncanny with the daemonic and the folklore malice the dead bear to the living. Dummies, mentioned affectionately in *Daphne*, were a relic of Nesbit's own childhood play. Nesbit whips up their scariness in *The Enchanted Castle* with some relish. She never stopped being tortured by her own fears. Her adult horror stories highlight heroes in near-death entombment and the malevolence of the dead, reminiscent of the Bordeaux mummies that had frightened her as a child. Fear appears to be the reverse of Nesbit's craving for fantasy, as addictive, mesmerizing, destructive and inspirational.

In the end the ring loses its magic, to become a normal wedding ring. Treasures it once created vanish; large chunks of the castle have to be rebuilt at great expense. Life without magic, Nesbit suggests, is mundane; the exercise of imagination is the province of childhood, not adulthood. Lord Yalding believes he is mad when he meets the children and the ring's magic. Jimmy, childishly wishing to be rich, is turned into a mean, fat, elderly, prosperous stockbroker, only interested in money. While Nesbit's mockery of capitalism borders on the anti-Semitic – the Queen of Babylon, let loose in London, has the entire Stock Exchange felled by Babylonian guards ('Henry Hirsh is down now, and Prentice is cut in two...and there goes Lionel Cohen with his head off...')[95] and Mr Levinstein hates to see the poor feasting on the Queen's delicious food – her real dislike is of aging. Jimmy, and the Lamb in *Five Children and It* who has a similar disagreeable-grown-up transformation spell, confirm her belief that though children are essentially foolish, and childhood a time of limitations, only the childlike enjoy freedom. Her books, like her life, show that imagination brings excitement, insurrection, fun, bliss and despair, and though imagination is fraught with risk, only the dull would be swayed by safety.

Notes

CHAPTER 1. INTRODUCTION: THREADS IN THE TAPESTRY

1. Judith Plotz, *Romanticism and the Vocation of Childhood* (New York: Palgrave, 2001), 13.
2. Quoted in Kathleen Tillotson et al., 'Charlotte Yonge as a Critic of Literature', in *'A Chaplet for Charlotte Yonge* (London: Cresset Press, 1965), 59; orig. in 'Children's Literature of the Last Century', *Macmillan's Magazine*, vol. 20 (July-September, 1869).
3. Mrs. Sherwood, *The Fairchild Family* (London: George Routledge & Sons, Ltd, n.d.), 26, 31, 50, 65, 136 etc).
4. Henry Mayhew, *London Labour and the London Poor* (London: Penguin, 1985).
5. O. F. Walton, *A Peep Behind the Scenes* (publication details ??????).
6. Kimberley Reynolds, *Girls Only?* (London: Harvester Wheatsheaf, (1990), 94.
7. Walter Houghton, *The Victorian Frame of Mind* (New Haven and London: Yale University Press, 1985), 187.
8. Frances Hodgson Burnett, *The One I Knew Best of All* (London: Warne 1905), 161.
9. Houghton, *Victorian Frame of Mind*, 192.
10. Edward Salmon, 'Literature for the Little Ones' (1887), in Lance Salway (ed.), *A Peculiar Gift: Nineteenth Century Writings on Books for Children* (London: Kestral, 1976), 47.
11. R. Lancelyn Green, *Tellers of Tales* (London: Edmund Ward, 1946; rev. edn 1965), 58.
12. Ibid.
13. *Manchester Guardian*, 20 September 1905.
14. M. Molesworth, 'On the Art of Writing Fiction for Children', *Atalanta*, 1893.
15. David Davidson, *Memories of a Long Life* (Edinburgh: David Douglas, 1893), 320.
16. Sally Mitchell, *Dinah Mulock Craik* (Boston, Twayne: 1983), 8.
17. John Ruskin, 'Of Queens' Gardens', in *Sesame and Lilies* (London: Milner and Co. Ltd, n.d.).

18. Virginia Woolf, *Killing the Angel in the House* (London: Penguin, 1995), 3.
19. Dinah Mulock Craik, *A Woman's Thoughts about Women* (London: Hurst and Blacket, 1858), 50.
20. Jenny Uglow, *Elizabeth Gaskell* (London: Faber and Faber, 1993), 45.
21. Ibid., 317.
22. Lucasta Miller, *The Brontë Myth* (London: Jonathan Cape, 2001), 19.
23. Charlotte Yonge, 'Children's Literature of the Last Century', *Macmillan's Magazine*, 1869, 229
24. Gertrude Slater, *Journal of Education*, 1897, in Salway (ed.), *A Peculiar Gift*.
25. Mary Poovey, *Uneven Developments* (London: Virago, 1989), 89.
26. M. Molesworth, 'Story Writing', *Monthly Packet*, 1894, 164.
27. Julia Briggs, 'Women Writers and Writing for Children', in G. Avery and J. Briggs (eds), *Children and Their Books* (Oxford: Clarendon Press, 1989), 245.
28. E. Nesbit, *Long Ago When I Was Young* (London: Beehive Books, 1987).

CHAPTER 2. JULIANA HORATIA EWING

1. Marghanita Laski, *Mrs Ewing, Mrs Molesworth and Mrs Hodgson Burnett* (London: Arthur Barker Ltd, 1950), 55.
2. Christabel Maxwell, *Mrs Gatty and Mrs Ewing* (London: Constable, 1949), 149.
3. Ibid.,16.
4. Ibid., 96.
5. Ibid., 138.
6. Gatty, Margaret, *Aunt Judy's Tales* (London: Bell and Daldy, 1861), 140.
7. Maxwell, *Mrs Gatty and Mrs Ewing*, 82.
8. Ibid., 157.
9. Sanjay Sircar, 'The Victorian "Auntly" Narrative Voice and Mrs Molesworth's Cuckoo Clock', *Children's Literature*, 17 (1989).
10. Mrs Gatty, *Aunt Judy's Tales* (London: Bell & Daldry, 1861),2.
11. M. Molesworth, 'Mrs Ewing's Less Well-Known Books', *Contemporary Review*, March 1886.
12. Margaret Blom and Thomas Blom (eds), *Canada Home* (Vancouver: University of British Columbia Press, 1983), 245.
13. Maxwell, *Mrs Gatty and Mrs Ewing*, 17
14. Ethel Smyth, *Impressions That Remained* (London: Longmans, Green & Co., 1919), 112.
15. Blom and Blom (eds), *Canada Home*, 162.

16. Ibid., 188.
17. Ibid., 188.
18. Ibid., 189.
19. Ibid., 284.
20. Ibid., 173.
21. Ibid., 218.
22. Ibid., 219.
23. Ibid., 118.
24. Ibid., 193.
25. Ibid., 192.
26. Horatia Gatty, *Juliana Horatia Ewing and Her Books* (London: SPCK, 1896), 32.
27. Gillian Avery, *Mrs Ewing* (London: Bodley Head, 1961), 7.
28. Smyth, *Impressions That Remained*, 112.
29. Elaine Showalter, *The Female Malady* (London: Virago, 1987), 5.
30. Mary Poovey, *Uneven Developments* (London: Virago, 1989), 36.
31. Stanley Weintraub, *Four Rossettis: A Victorian Biography* (London: Allen, 1977), 17.
32. Maxwell, *Mrs Gatty and Mrs Ewing*, 242.
33. Ibid., 241.
34. Gillian Avery, *Nineteenth-Century Children* (London: Hodder & Stoughton, 1965), 151.
35. Gillian Avery, *Mrs Ewing* (London: Bodley Head, 1961), 38.
36. Laski, *Mrs Ewing, Mrs Molesworth and Mrs Hodgson Burnett*, 52.
37. Maxwell, *Mrs Gatty and Mrs Ewing*, 245.
38. M. Molesworth, 'Mrs Ewing's Less Well-Known Books', in *Studies and Stories* (London: A. D. Innes, 1893).
39. Charlotte Yonge, 'What Books to Lend and What to Give', in R. Lancelyn Green, *Tellers of Tales* (London: Edmund Ward, 1946; rev. edn 1965), 102.
40. Ibid., 103.
41. Houghton, *Victorian Frame of Mind*, 13.
42. *The Spectator*, 4 January 1896.
43. Rudyard Kipling, *Something of Myself* (London: Macmillan, 1937), 7.
44. Kathryn Hughes, *The Victorian Governess* (London: Hambledon Press, 1993), 61.
45. Ibid.
46. Carol Dyhouse, *Girls Growing Up in Late Victorian and Edwardian England* (London: Routledge & Kegan Paul, 1981), 42.
47. Jack Zipes, *Fairy Tales and the Art of Subversion* (New York: Routledge, 1991), 101.
48. Ibid.
49. J. H. Ewing, *Old Fashioned Fairy Tales* (London: Bell & Daldy, 1882), xiv.

50. Blom and Blom (eds), *Canada Home*, 257
51. Ewing, *Old Fashioned Fairy Tales*, vi.
52. Houghton, *Victorian Frame of Mind*, 255.
53. Christina Rossetti, *The Poetical Works of Christina Georgina Rosetti* (London: Macmillan,1911), 278.

CHAPTER 3. MARY LOUISA MOLESWORTH

1. *The Times*, 22 July 1921.
2. Salmon, 'Literature for the Little Ones', 46.
3. Jane Cooper, *Mrs Molesworth* (Sussex: Pratts Folly Press, 2002), 289.
4. Cooper, *Mrs Molesworth*, 291.
5. M. Molesworth, *The Carved Lions* (London: Macmillan, 1895), 2.
6. M. Molesworth, 'A Ramble around Childhood', *Girl's Own Annual*, 20 (1898–9).
7. M. Molesworth, 'On the Art of Writing Fiction for Children', *Atalanta*, 1893, 583.
8. Samuel Smiles, *Self-Help, with Illustrations of Conduct and Perseverence* (1859), (London: IEA Health and Welfare Unit, 1996), 239.
9. M. Molesworth, *Rosy* (London: Macmillan, 1882), 203.
10. M. Molesworth, *Jasper* (London: Macmillan, 1906), 203.
11. Ibid., 138.
12. M. Molesworth, *The Oriel Window* (London: Macmillan, 1896).
13. M. Molesworth, 'Story-Reading and Story-Writing', *Chamber's Journal*, 1887–8, 772.
14. Molesworth, 'On the Art of Writing Fiction for Children', 583.
15. Cooper,*Mrs Molesworth*, 82.
16. Letter from Molesworth to Warren, Christmas Eve, 1868.
17. Letter from Molesworth to Warren, 1 March 1868.
18. Letter from Molesworth to Warren, n.d., 1868.
19. Letter from Molesworth to Warren, 1 June 1868.
20. Cooper, *Mrs Molesworth*, 145.
21. Letter from Molesworth to Warren, 10 December 1868.
22. Cooper, *Mrs Molesworth*, 118.
23. M. Molesworth, *The Sealskin Purse*, in *Studies and Stories* (London: A. D. Innes, 1893), 146.
24. M. Molesworth, *Blanche* (London: Chambers, 1983).
25. M. Molesworth, *Silverthorns* (London: Hatchards, 1887).
26. M. Molesworth, *The Rectory Children* (London: Macmillan, 1885).
27. M. Molesworth, *Carrots* (London: Macmillan, 1876).
28. Molesworth, 'On the Art of Writing Fiction for Children', 583.
29. Roger Lancelyn Green, *Mrs Molesworth* (London: Bodley Head, 1961), 39.

30. Molesworth, *Carrots*, 92.
31. Ibid., 93.
32. Letter from Molesworth to Warren, n.d. [1870].
33. Letter from Molesworth to Warren, 3 March 1886.
34. Cooper, *Mrs Molesworth*, 193.
35. Ibid., 194.
36. Letter to Mr Craik, n.d.
37. Letter to Mr Macmillan, 17 January 1917.
38. Green, *Mrs Molesworth*, 47
39. M. Molesworth, *Marrying and Giving in Marriage* (London: Longmans, 1887), 12.
40. Cooper, *Mrs Molesworth*, 335.
41. Ibid., 221.
42. Green, *Mrs Molesworth*, 47.
43. Letter to Mr Craik, 22 February1888.
44. Cooper, *Mrs Molesworth*, 283
45. Ibid., 292.
46. Frances Hodgson Burnett leased 44 Lexham Gardens in 1889, but no evidence exists of their meeting or if Burnett, like Molesworth, found Kensington disappointing.
47. Letter to Mr Craik, 22 February1888.
48. Cooper, *Mrs Molesworth*, 235.
49. A. C., Swinburne, 'Charles Reade', *The Nineteenth Century*, vol. 16 (October 1884), 563.
50. Cooper, *Mrs Molesworth*, 341.
51. M.-J. Lancaster (ed.), *Letters of Engagement, The Love Letters of Adrian Hope and Laura Troubridge* (London: Tite Street Press, 2002), 418.
52. Ibid., 424.
53. Cooper, *Mrs Molesworth*, 328.
54. *Sunday Times*, 24 July 1921.
55. Cooper, *Mrs Molesworth*, 328.
56. M. Molesworth, *Grandmother Dear* (London: Macmillan, 1878), 73.
57. Salmon, 'Literature for the Little Ones', 61.
58. Gertrude Slater 'Concerning Children's Books', in Salway (ed.), *A Peculiar Gift*, 348.
59. The Westminster Budget, October 1893.
60. Sircar, S., *The Lion and the Unicorn*, vol. 121 (1997).
61. Sally Mitchell, *The New Girl* (New York: Columbia University Press, 1995).
62. Carol Dyhouse, *Girls Growing Up in Late Victorian and Edwardian England* (London: Routledge and Kegan Paul, 1981), 159.
63. Cooper, *Mrs Molesworth*, 135.
64. Letter to Mr Craik, 4 March 1908.
65. M. Forster, *Good Wives* (London: Vintage, 2002), 92.

66. Christabel Coleridge, quoted in S. Foster and J. Simons, *What Katy Read* (London: Macmillan, 1995), 65.
67. L. Nead, *Myths of Sexuality* (Oxford: Blackwell, 1988), 6.
68. K. Reynolds and N. Humble, *Victorian Heroines* (London: Harvester Wheatsheaf, 1993), 18.
69. S. Mitchell, *The New Girl*, 151.
70. Molesworth, 'On the Art of Writing Fiction for Children', 345.
71. Salmon, 'Literature for the Little Ones', in Salway, *A Peculiar Gift*, 60.
72. 'On the Art of Writing Fiction for Children', 341.
73. Jack Zipes, *Fairy Tales and the Art of Subversion* (New York: Routledge, 1983), 172.
74. M. Molesworth, 'Story-Reading and Story-Writing', 772.

CHAPTER 4. FRANCES HODGSON BURNETT

1. Frances Hodgson Burnett, *Through One Administration* (London: Warne, 1883), 73.
2. Anne Thwaite, *Waiting for the Party* (London: Secker & Warburg, 1974), 76.
3. Frances Hodgson Burnett, *The One I Knew Best of All* (London: Warne, 1893), 214.
4. Ibid., 124.
5. Frances Hodgson Burnett, *A Little Princess* (London, Warne, 1905), 140.
6. Burnett, *The One I Knew Best of All*, 82.
7. Phyllis Bixler, *Frances Hodgson Burnett* (Boston: Twayne, 1984), 123.
8. Burnett, *The One I Knew Best of All*, 78.
9. Ibid., 229.
10. Ibid., 246.
11. Ibid., 251.
12. Thwaite, *Waiting for the Party*, 38.
13. Frances Hodgson Burnett, 'How I Served My Apprenticeship', *Lady's Realm*, 1896.
14. Thwaite, *Waiting for the Party*, 50.
15. M. Keyser, 'Quite Contrary": Frances Hodgson Burnett's *The Secret Garden', Children's Literature*, vol. 11, 11.
16. Ibid.
17. Gretchen Gerzina, *Frances Hodgson Burnett* (London: Chatto & Windus, 2004), 59.
18. Marghanita Laski, *Mrs Ewing, Mrs Molesworth and Mrs Hodgson Burnett* (London: Arthur Barker, Ltd, 1950), 79.
19. Bixler, *Frances Hodgson Burnett*, 123.
20. Burnett, *Through One Administration*, 20.

21. Gerzina, *Frances Hodgson Burnett*, 28.
22. Bixler, *Frances Hodgson Burnett*, 123.
23. Thwaite, *Waiting for the Party*, 81
24. Frances Hodgson Burnett, 'How Fauntleroy Occurred', in *The Captain's Youngest, Piccino and Other Child Stories* (London: Warne, 1894), 123.
25. Ibid., 144.
26. Ibid., 157.
27. Frances Hodgson Burnett, *Two Little Pilgrims Progress* (London: Warne, 1895), 215.
28. Frances Hodgson Burnett, *The Shuttle* (London: Heinemann, 1907), 44.
29. Ibid., 51.
30. Thwaite, *Waiting for the Party*, 176.
31. Ibid., 192.
32. Ibid., 193.
33. Gerzina, *Frances Hodgson Burnett*, 217.
34. Thwaite, *Waiting for the Party*, 237.
35. Ibid.
36. Gerzina, *Frances Hodgson Burnett*, 219.
37. Burnett, *The Shuttle*, 238.
38. Frances Hodgson Burnett, *The Secret Garden* (London, Heinemann, 1911), 216.
39. M. Laski, Introduction to Frances Hodgson Burnett, *The Making of a Marchioness* (1901) (London: Anthony Blond, 1966), 28.
40. Ibid., 29.
41. Ibid., 52
42. Frances Hodgson Burnett, *The White People* (London: Heinemann, 1920).
43. Gerzina, *Frances Hodgson Burnett*, 88.
44. Alex Owen, *The Darkened Room: Women, Power and Spiritualism in late Victorian England* (London: Virago, 1988).
45. Thwaite, *Waiting for the Party*, 88.
46. Burnett, *The Shuttle*, 358.
47. Frances Hodgson Burnett, *The Dawn of a Tomorrow* (London: Warne, 1907), 90.
48. Frances Hodgson Burnett, *Land of the Blue Flower* (London: Putnam, 1912).
49. Burnett, *The Secret Garden*, 289.
50. Thwaite, *Waiting for the Party*, 23.
51. Ibid., 9.
52. Hodgson Burnett, Frances, *The Captain's Youngest, Piccino and Other Child Stories* (London: Warne, 1894).
53. Magdalen Goffin, *Maria Pasqua* (Oxford: Oxford University Press, 1979).

54. Burnett, *Little Lord Fauntleroy* (London: Warne, 1883), 86.
55. Ibid., 90.
56. Ibid., 87.
57. Phyllis Bixler, 'Tradition and the Individual Talent of Frances Hodgson Burnett', *Children's Literature*, 7 (1978), 191–207.
58. H. Carpenter and M. Pritchard, *The Oxford Companion to Children's Literature* (Oxford: Oxford University Press, 1984), 316.
59. Frances Hodgson Burnett, *Sara Crewe* (London: Fisher Unwin, 1887), 11.
60. Burnett, *A Little Princess*, 94.
61. Ibid., 44.
62. Ibid., 39.
63. E. R. Gruner, 'Role Moldels in *A Little Princess*', *The Lion and the Unicorn*, 2 (1998), 163.
64. Hodgson Burnett associated dark hair with driven heroines; see also Meg in *Two Little Pilgrims' Progress* and Betty in *The Shuttle*.
65. Burnett, *A Little Princess*, 9.
66. Ibid., 180.
67. Ibid., 21.
68. Bixler, *Frances Hodgson Burnett*, 13.
69. A. Lurie, (London: Penguin, 1999), xiv.
70. H. Carpenter, *Secret The Secret Garden Gardens* (London: George Allen & Unwin, 1985).
71. P. Acroyd, *Albion: The Origins of the English Imagination* (London: Chatto & Windus, 2002), 411.
72. Burnett, *The Secret Garden*, 236.
73. Ibid., 187.
74. K. Reynolds and N. Humble, *Victorian Heroines: Representatives of Femininity in Nineteenth-Century Literature and Art* (New York: Harvester Wheatsheaf, 1993).
75. L. Peters, *Orphan Texts* (Manchester: Manchester University Texts, 2000).
76. Bixler, *Frances Hodgson Burnett*, 1984.
77. Thwaite, *Waiting for the Party*, 125.
78. Keyser, ' "Quite Contrary" ', 11.
79. Burnett, *The Secret Garden*, 183.
80. Lurie, *The Secret Garden*, xxiv.
81. Burnett, *The Secret Garden*, 78.
82. Ibid., 79.
83. Ibid., 203.
84. Ibid., 70.
85. Ibid., 90.
86. J. Plotz, 'Secret Garden II or *Lady Chatterley's Lover* as Palimpsest', *Children's Literature Association Quarterly*, vols 19–20 (1994–6).

CHAPTER 5. EDITH NESBIT

1. H. Carpenter, *Secret Gardens* (London: George Allen & Unwin, 1985), 135.
2. Alfred H. Miles, *The Poets and Poetry of the Century*, vol. 8 (London: Hutchinson, 1892), 579–80.
3. E. Nesbit, *The Story of the Treasure Seekers* (London: T. Fisher Unwin, 1899), 51.
4. E. Nesbit, *Long Ago When I Was Young* (London: Beehive Books, 1966), 29.
5. E. Nesbit, *Wings and the Child* (London: Hodder & Stoughton, 1913), 39.
6. Nesbit, *Long Ago When I Was Young*, 56
7. Ibid., 40.
8. Ibid., 77.
9. Ibid., 61.
10. Doris Langley Moore, *E. Nesbit* (London: Ernest Benn, 1933), 75.
11. Nesbit, *Long Ago When I Was Young*, 27.
12. Nesbit, *Wings and the Child*, 175.
13. 'On the Art of Writing Fiction for Children', *Atalanta*, 1893, 583.
14. Julia Briggs, *A Woman of Passion* (London: Hutchinson, 1987), 67.
15. E. Nesbit, *Wet Magic* (London: T. Werner Laurie, 1913).
16. Ibid., 188.
17. Ibid., 185.
18. Nesbit, *Long Ago When I Was Young*, 127
19. E. Nesbit, *The New Treasure Seekers* (London: T. Fisher Unwin, 1904), 565.
20. E. Nesbit, *The Red House* (London: Methuen, 1902), 76.
21. Nesbit, *Long Ago When I Was Young*, 112.
22. Lovat Dixon, *H. G. Wells* (London: Macmillan, 1971), 30.
23. E. Nesbit, *Daphne in Fitzroy Street* (London: George Allen & Sons, 1909), 54.
24. Hesketh Pearson, *Bernard Shaw* (London: Collins, 1942), 117.
25. Nesbit, *Daphne in Fitzroy Street*, 371.
26. Ibid., 366.
27. Ibid., 404.
28. Briggs, *A Woman of Passion*, 100.
29. Ibid., 104.
30. Nesbit, *Daphne in Fitzroy Street*, 367.
31. Nesbit, *Wings and the Child*, 87.
32. Berta Ruck, *A Smile for the Past* (London: Hutchinson, 1959), 120.
33. Briggs, *A Woman of Passion*, 112.
34. Ibid., 114.

35. Nesbit, *The New Treasure Seekers*, 565.
36. Ibid., 37.
37. E. Nesbit, *Five of Us and Madelaine* (London: T. Fisher Unwin, 1925), 53.
38. Dixon, *H. G. Wells*, 131.
39. Ruck, *A Smile for the Past*, 115.
40. Ibid., 115.
41. Briggs, *A Woman of Passion*, 154.
42. Ruck, *A Smile for the Past*, 117.
43. Briggs, *A Woman of Passion*, 208.
44. Moore, *E. Nesbit*, 189.
45. Ibid., 180.
46. M. Stetz, ' "The Mighty Mother cannot bring thee in"': E. Nesbit in the Wilderness', *Victorian Poetry*, vol. 33 (Summer 1995), West Virginia University.
47. Nesbit, *Wings and the Child*, 6.
48. Briggs, *A Woman of Passion*, 371.
49. Ruck, *A Smile for the Past*, 119.
50. Briggs, *A Woman of Passion*, 378.
51. Ruck, *A Smile for the Past*, 120.
52. Ibid., 122.
53. Ibid., 121.
54. Peter Coveney, *The Image of Childhood* (London: Penguin, 1967), 241.
55. E. Nesbit, *Nine Unlikely Tales* (London: T. Fisher Unwin, 1901).
56. Nesbit, *Wet Magic*, 9.
57. E. Nesbit, *The Railway Children*, London, Wells Gardner Darton, 1906, 20
58. Ibid., 62.
59. Nesbit, *The Story of the Treasure Seekers*, 56.
60. E. Nesbit, *The Enchanted Castle* (London, T. Fisher Unwin, 1907), 21.
61. E. Nesbit, *Five Children and It* (London: T. Fisher Unwin, 1902), 231.
62. Ibid., 156.
63. John Stephens, *Language and Ideology in Children's Fiction* (London: Longman, 1992), 128.
64. Nesbit, *Five Children and It*, 6.
65. D. Newsome, *The Victorian World Picture* (London: Murray, 1997).
66. Harry Graham, *Ruthless Rhymes for Heartless Homes* (London: Edward Arnold, 1899), 18.
67. G. Battiscombe, *Queen Alexandra* (London: Constable, 1969), 126.
68. Nesbit, *The Red House*, 176.
69. Ibid., 180.
70. E. Nesbit, *The Wouldbegoods* (London: T. Fisher Unwin, 1901), 460.
71. Nesbit, *The New Treasure Seekers*, 569.
72. Ibid., 575.

73. Nesbit, *The Story of the Treasure Seekers*, 56.
74. Nesbit, *The Wouldbegoods*, 392.
75. Ibid., 233.
76. Julia Briggs, 'Women Writers: Sarah Fielding to E. Nesbit', in G. Avery and J. Briggs, *Children and Their Books* (Oxford: Clarendon Press, 1989), 139.
77. E. Nesbit, *The Story of the Amulet* (London: T. Fisher Unwin, 1906), 138.
78. E. Nesbit, *The House of Arden* (London: T. Fisher Unwin, 1908), 138.
79. Nesbit, *The Story of the Treasure Seekers*, 138.
80. Nesbit, *The Railway Children*, 186.
81. Nesbit, *The New Treasure Seekers*, 628.
82. Nesbit, *The Railway Children*, 186.
83. Ibid., 15.
84. Ibid., 11.
85. Ibid., 201–2.
86. Ibid., 202.
87. S. Foster and J. Symons, *What Katy Read* (London: Macmillan, 1995), 137.
88. Nesbit, *The Railway Children*, 17.
89. Ibid., 167.
90. Ibid., 89.
91. Ibid., 135.
92. Ibid., 18.
93. Ibid., 168.
94. Nesbit, E. *The Enchanted Castle* (London: T. Fisher Unwin, 1907), 137.
95. Nesbit, *The Story of the Amulet*, 136.

Bibliography

JULIANA HORATIA EWING

Selected works by Mrs Ewing

(The dates in square brackets are the dates of first publication in magazines.)

Mrs Overtheway's Remembrances (London: Bell, 1869) [1866–8].
The Brownies and Other Tales (London: Bell, 1870) [*The Brownies*, 1865; *The Land of Lost Toys*, 1869; *Amelia and the Dwarfs*, 1870].
A Flat Iron for a Farthing (London: Bell, 1872) [1870–71].
Lob-Lie-by-the-Fire (London: Bell, 1874).
Six to Sixteen (London: Bell, 1875) [1872].
Jackanapes (London: SPCK, 1883) [1879].
Daddy Darwin's Dovecote (London: SPCK, 1884) [1881].
The Story of a Short Life (London: SPCK, 1885) [1882].

Biography and criticism

Ewing's papers are held in the archives of the Sheffield Library. Gatty family papers are held in the archives of Reading University.

Avery, Gillian, *Mrs Ewing* (London: Bodley Head, 1961).
Blom, M. and T. (eds), *Canada Home* (British Columbia: University of British Columbia, 1983).
Gatty, Horatia K. F., *Juliana Horatia Ewing and her Books* (London: SPCK, 1896).
Jones, J. and M., *The Remarkable Gatty Family of Ecclesfield* (Rotherham: Green Tree Publications, 2003).
Laski, Marghanita, *Mrs Ewing, Mrs Molesworth and Mrs Hodgson Burnett* (London: Arthur Barker, 1950).
Maxwell, Christabel, *Mrs Gatty and Mrs Ewing* (London: Constable, 1949).
Molesworth, Mrs, 'Mrs Ewing's Less Well-Known Books', in *Studies and Stories* (London: A. D. Innes, 1893).

Smyth, Dame Ethel, *Impressions that Remained*, 2 vols (Longmans, Green & Co., 1919).

MARY LOUISA MOLESWORTH

Selected works by Mrs Molesworth

Fiction

Tell Me a Story (London: Macmillan, 1875).
Carrots: Just a Little Boy (London: Macmillan, 1876).
The Cuckoo Clock (London: Macmillan, 1877).
Grandmother Dear (London: Macmillan, 1878).
Rosy (London: Macmillan, 1882).
Marrying and Giving in Marriage (London: Longmans, 1887).
The Rectory Children (London: Macmillan 1889).
The Old Pincushion (London: Griffith Farran, 1889).
Sweet Content (London: Griffith Farran, 1891).
Studies and Stories (London: A. D. Innes 1893).
Blanche (London: Chambers, 1893).
Sheila's Mystery (London: Macmillan, 1895).
Fairy Stories, ed. Roger Lancelyn Green (London: Harvill, 1957).

Articles

'On the art of Writing Fiction for Children', *Atalanta*, May 1893.
'How I Write My Children's Stories', *Little Folks*, July 1894.
'Story-Writing', *Monthly Packet*, August 1894.
'Story-Reading and Story-Writing', *Chamber's Journal*, November 1898.

Biography and criticism

Cooper, Jane, *Mrs Molesworth* (Sussex: Pratt's Folly Press, 2002).
Fisher, Margery, 'Stories from a Victorian Nursery', *Signal*, 69 (September 1992).
Green, Roger Lancelyn, *Mrs Molesworth* (London: Bodley Head, 1961).
——, *Tellers of Tales: Children's Books and Authors from 1800 to 1968* (London: Edmund Ward, 1946; rev. edn 1965).
Moss, Anita, 'Mrs Molesworth: Victorian Visionary', *The Lion and the Unicorn*, June 1998.
Sebag-Montefiore, Mary, 'Nice Girls Don't (But Want To): Work Ethic Conflicts and Conundrums in Mrs Molesworth's Books for Girls', *The Lion and the Unicorn*, September 2002.
Sircar, Sanjay, 'The Victorian "Auntly" Narrative Voice and Mrs Molesworth's Cuckoo Clock', *Children's Literature*, 17 (1989).

FRANCES HODGSON BURNETT

Selected works by Frances Hodgson Burnett

Fiction

That Lass O'Lowrie's (New York: Scribner, 1877; London: Warne, 1877).

Through One Administration (Boston: Osgood, 1883; London: Warne, 1883).

Little Lord Fauntleroy (New York: Scribner, 1886; London: Warne, 1886).

Sara Crewe (New York: Scribner, 1888; London: Fisher Unwin, 1887).

Editha's Burglar (Boston: Jordon Marsh, 1888; London: Warne, 1888).

The Real Little Lord Fauntleroy (play), Terry's Theatre, London, May 1888; Broadway Theater, New York, December 1888.

Little Saint Elizabeth and Other Stories (New York: Scribner, 1890; London: Warne 1890).

Nixie (play; from *Editha's Burglar*), Terry's Theatre, London, April, 1890.

The One I Knew Best of All (New York: Scribner, 1893; London: Warne, 1893).

Piccino and Other Child Stories (New York: Scribner, 1894; London: Warne, 1893).

The Two Little Pilgrims' Progress (New York: Scribner, 1895; London: Warne, 1895).

The Making of a Marchioness (New York: Stokes, 1901; London: Smith, Elder & Co., 1901).

A Little Princess (play; originally *A Little Unfairy Princess*), Shaftsbury Theatre, London, December 1902; Criterion Theatre, January 1903.

In a Closed Room (New York: McClure, 1905; London: Hodder, 1904).

A Little Princess (New York: Scribner, 1905; London: Warne, 1905).

The Dawn of a Tomorrow (New York: Scribner, 1906; London: Warne, 1907).

The Shuttle (New York: Stokes, 1907; London: Heinemann, 1907).

The Secret Garden (New York: Stokes, 1911; London: Heinemann, 1911).

The White People (New York: Harper, 1917; London: Heinemann, 1920).

Articles

'How I Served my Apprenticeship', *Lady's Realm*, 1896.

Biography and criticism

Bixler, Phyllis, *Frances Hodgson Burnett*, Twayne's English Authors (Boston: K. Hall, 1984).

——, 'Tradition and the Individual Talent of Frances Hodgson Burnett: A Generic Analysis of *Little Lord Fauntleroy*, *A Little Princess* and *The*

Secret Garden', *Children's Literature*, 7 (1978), 191–207.

Gerzina, Gretchen, *Frances Hodgson Burnett* (London: Chatto & Windus, 2004).

Gruner, E. R., 'Role Models in *A Little Princess*', *The Lion and the Unicorn*, 2 (1998), 163.

Keyser, E. L., 'Quite Contrary: Frances Hodgson Burnett's *The Secret Garden*', *Children's Literature*, 2 (1983), 1–13.

Lurie, Alison, Introduction, in Frances Hodgson Burnett, *The Secret Garden*, ed. A. Lurie (London: Penguin, 1999), xiv.

Plotz, J., 'Secret Garden 11; or Lady Chatterley's Lover as Palimpsest', *Children's Literature Association Quarterly*, 19–20 (1994–6).

Thwaite, Anne, *Waiting for the Party* (London: Secker & Warburg, 1974).

EDITH NESBIT

Selected works by E. Nesbit

The Poets and the Poetry of the Century, ed. Alfred H. Mile (London: Hutchinson, 1891).

The Story of the Treasure Seekers (London: Fisher Unwin, 1899).

The Book of Dragons (London: Harper & Bros, 1899).

Nine Unlikely Tales for Children (London: Fisher Unwin, 1901).

The Wouldbegoods (London: Fisher Unwin, 1901).

Five Children and It (London: Fisher Unwin, 1902).

The Red House (London: Methuen & Co, 1902).

The Phoenix and the Carpet (London: George Newnes, 1904).

The New Treasure Seekers (London: Fisher Unwin, 1904).

The Story of the Amulet (London: Fisher Unwin, 1906).

The Railway Children (London: Wells, Gardner, Darton & Co, 1906).

The Enchanted Castle (London: Fisher Unwin, 1907).

The House of Arden (London: Fisher Unwin, 1908).

Harding's Luck (London: Hodder & Stoughton, 1909).

Daphne in Fitzroy Street (London: George Allen & Sons, 1909).

The Magic City (London: Macmillan & Co, 1910).

The Magic World (London: Macmillan & Co. 1912).

Wet Magic (London: T. Werner Laurie, 1913).

Wings and the Child, or The Building of Magic Cities (London: Hodder & Stoughton, 1913).

Five of Us, and Madeline (London: Fisher Unwin, 1925) (posthumous).

Long Ago When I Was Young (posthumous; London: Whiting & Wheaton, 1966; Beehive, 1987).

Biography and criticism

Briggs, Julia, *A Woman of Passion: The Life of E. Nesbit* (London: Hutchinson, 1987).

Dickson, Lovat, *H. G. Wells* (London: Macmillan, 1971).

Green, Roger Lancelyn, *Tellers of Tales: Children's Books and Authors from 1800 to 1968* (London: Edmund Ward, 1946; rev. edn 1965).

Moore, Doris Langley, *E. Nesbit: A Biography* (London: Ernest Benn, 1933).

Ruck, Berta, *A Smile for the Past* (London: Hutchinson, 1959).

Stetz, M., 'E. Nesbit in the Wilderness', *Victorian Poetry*, 33 (Summer 1995).

Streatfield, Noel, *Magic and the Magician: E. Nesbit and her Children's Books* (London: Ernest Benn, 1958).

GENERALLY RELEVANT WORKS

Avery, Gillian, *Nineteenth-Century Children: Heroes and Heroines in English Children's Stories 1780–1900* (London: Hodder & Stoughton, 1965).

——, *Childhood's Pattern: A Study of the Heroes and Heroines of Children's Fiction, 1770–1950* (London: Hodder & Stoughton, 1975).

Calder, Jenni, *The Victorian Home* (London: Batsford, 1977).

Carpenter, Humphrey, *The Oxford Companion to Children's Literature* (Oxford: Oxford University Press, 1984).

——, *Secret Gardens* (London: George Allen & Unwin, 1985).

Clive, Mary Katharine, *The Day of Reckoning* (London: Macmillan & Co. Ltd, 1964).

Coveney, Peter, *The Image of Childhood* (London: Penguin, 1967).

Crook, J. Mordaunt, *The Rise of the Nouveaux Riches* (London: John Murray, 1999).

Cutt, Margaret Nancy, *Mrs Sherwood and her Books for Children* (London: Oxford University Press, 1974).

Dyhouse, Carol, *Girls Growing Up in Late Victorian and Edwardian England* (London: Routledge and Keegan Paul, 1981).

Foster, S. and J. Simons, *What Katy Read* (London: Macmillan, 1995).

Green, Roger Lancelyn, *Tellers of Tales: Children's Books and Authors from 1800 to 1968* (London: Edmund Ward, 1946; rev. edn 1965).

Hayter, Alethea, *Charlotte Younge*, Writers and their Work (Plymouth: Northcote House Publishers Ltd, 1996).

Horn, Pamela, *The Rise and Fall of the Victorian Servant* (Dublin: Gill & Macmillan, 1975).

Houghton, Walter, *The Victorian Frame of Mind, 1830–1870* (New Haven and London: Yale University Press, 1957).

Hughes, Kathryn, *The Victorian Governess* (London: Hambledon Press, 1993).

Laski, Marghanita, *Mrs Ewing, Mrs Molesworth, and Mrs Hodgson Burnett* (London: Arthur Barker, 1950).

Lochhead, Marion, *The Renaissance of Wonder in Children's Literature* (Edinburgh: Canongate, 1977).

Lurie, Alison, *Not in Front of the Grown-Ups* (London: Bloomsbury, 1990).

Mitchell, Sally, *The New Girl: Girl's Culture in England, 1880–1915* (New York: Methuen, 1985).

Newsome, D., *The Victorian World Picture* (London: Murray, 1997).

Peters, L., *Orphan Texts* (Manchester: Manchester University Press, 2000).

Plotz, Judith, *Romanticism and the Vocation of Childhood* (New York: Palgrave, 2001).

Poovey, Mary, *Uneven Developments: The Ideological Work of Gender in Mid-Victorian England* (London: Virago, 1989).

Reynolds, K., *Girls Only? Gender and Popular Girls' Fiction in Britain, 1880–1910* (London: Harvester Wheatsheaf, 1990).

——, *Children's Literature in the 1890s and the 1990s*, Writers and their Work (Plymouth: Northcote House Publishers Ltd, 1994).

Reynolds, K., and N. Humble, *Victorian Heroines: Representations of Femininity in Nineteenth-Century Literature and Art* (London: Harvester Wheatsheaf, 1993).

Salway, Lance (ed.), *A Peculiar Gift: Nineteenth Century Writings on Books for Children* (Harmondsworth: Kestrel, 1976).

Showalter, Elaine, *The Female Malady: Women, Madness and English Culture, 1830-1890* (London: Virago, 1987).

Smiles, Samuel, *Self-Help with Illustrations of Conduct and Perseverence* (London: IEA Health and Welfare Unit, 1866; repr. 1996).

St George, E. A. W., *The Descent of Manners: Etiquette, Rules & the Victorians* (London: Chatto & Windus, 1993).

Thwaite, M. F., *From Primer to Pleasure: An Introduction to the History of Children's Books in England from the Invention of Printing to 1900* (London: Library Association, 1963).

Wilson, A. N., *The Victorians* (London: Arrow Books, 2002).

Zipes, Jack (ed.), *Victorian Fairy Tales: The Revolt of the Fairies and Elves* (New York and London: Routledge, 1989).

Index

Printed in the United Kingdom
by Lightning Source UK Ltd.
127208UK00001B/619-645/A